Current Titles

Concepts in the Social Sciences

Populism

Paul Taggart

Open University Press
Buckingham · Philadelphia

Open University Press
Celtic Court
22 Ballmoor
Buckingham
MK18 1XW

email: enquiries@openup.co.uk
world wide web: www.openup.co.uk

and 325 Chestnut Street
Philadelphia, PA 19106, USA

First Published 2000

A catalogue record of this book is available from the British Library

ISBN 0 335 20045 1 (pbk)   0 335 20046 X (hbk)

Library of Congress Cataloging-in-Publication Data
Taggart, Paul A.
   Populism / Paul Taggart.
      p.   cm. — (Concepts in the social sciences.)
   Includes bibliographical references and index.
   ISBN 0-335-20046-X (hb) — ISBN 0-335-20045-1 (pbk.)
   1. Democracy. 2. Populism. 3. Social movements. I. Title. II. Series.
JC423.T252 2000
320.51′3—dc21   99-086747

Typeset by Type Study, Scarborough, North Yorkshire
Printed in Great Britain by St Edmundsbury Press, Bury St Edmunds, Suffolk

Contents

Preface

This book came out of an attempt to answer a simple enquiry from my parents Keith and Pat Taggart, as to what one of the words in the title of my last book meant. It was a simple enough question. The answer has not been as straightforward as the question. In coming to an answer, I have come to believe that the study of populism has suffered from being fractured. Each case of populism has been pored over, but usually in isolation. I have therefore attempted to write a book that brings the pieces together. Being serious about populism requires investment. I hope the brevity of the book makes this investment less taxing for the reader.

I am grateful for the support of colleagues at the University of Sussex, especially those in the Sussex European Institute, the International Relations and Politics group and the School of Social Sciences, for the patience of the Open University Press, and for the unflagging support of Bhavna Sapat. I owe a huge debt to Bruce Graham whose influence on the book has gone way beyond advice, conversation and critique and has found its way on to all the pages in one form or another (not least in the terms used in Chapter 8), but who is not responsible for the content of those pages. I am deeply grateful for his help and for the pleasure of so many conversations about the subject.

1
Introduction

Populism is an unusual concept. Look at anything closely enough for a period of time and it will begin to seem unusual, but even the most cursory of glances at populism shows it to be out of the ordinary. Populism has many of the attributes of an ideology, but not all of them. At times, it has had great resonance across the world, and yet at other times it has been inconsequential. It has an essential impalpability, an awkward conceptual slipperiness. For different sets of people it veers between having great meaning and fundamental vacuousness. For elites it is both an object of fascination and a phenomenon of great distaste and danger. To be catalysed into a political force it sometimes relies on great leaders and sometimes on great masses. Where it relies on leaders, it requires the most extraordinary individuals to lead the most ordinary of people. Appearing to be revolutionary, populism draws great support at times of crisis but, in practice, it is invariably reformist and incapable of offering fundamental 'root and branch' reform. It is episodic, appearing at times with great force and offering the potential to radically transform politics. But it soon dissipates. It is not without effect; when at its height, it invariably structures the content and tone of politics. Wherever there is representative politics, it is omnipresent as a potential movement or set of ideas to be drawn on by movements.

In short, the phenomena which observers and participants describe as populist are unlike movements which form parties, develop programmes and policies and lead relatively stable and patterned political lives. Populist movements have systems of belief which are diffuse; they are inherently difficult to control and organize; they lack consistency; and their activity waxes and wanes with a bewildering frequency. Populism is a difficult, slippery concept. It lacks features that would make it more tangible. Rooted in it are characteristics that render it quintessentially mercurial. For these reasons, it is profoundly difficult to construct a generalized description, let alone a universal and comprehensive definition, of populism as an idea or as a political movement.

Isaiah Berlin talked of the 'Cinderella complex' of populism, whereby we seek a perfect fit for the 'slipper' of populism, searching among the feet that nearly fit but always in search of the one true limb that will provide us with the pure case of populism (quoted in Allcock 1971: 385). The warning is clear: a search for the perfect fit for populism is both illusory and unsatisfying and will not lead to a happy ending.

Ernesto Laclau offers a similar warning about how populism can end up vanishing if we study it too closely. He describes a process whereby we start with the assumption that there is something called populism, so we define it, look for examples of it, study them, and then refine our definition so that it fits the examples we studied. When we seek to then give a general definition we resort to comparing the specificities of the movements but, because they fundamentally differ, we end up dropping populism (Laclau 1977: 145). This circularity is certainly a danger, and I am not sure it is one we can fully avoid.

I approach these problems in these pages by exploring six key themes that run through populism:

- populists as hostile to representative politics;
- populists identifying themselves with an idealized heartland within the community they favour;
- populism as an ideology lacking core values;
- populism as a powerful reaction to a sense of extreme crisis;
- populism as containing fundamental dilemmas that make it self-limiting;
- populism as a chameleon, adopting the colours of its environment.

The six themes are designed to be independent and capable of interacting with each other in different ways. Context is therefore important but should not blind us to the possibility of generalization. The possibility of generalization is an important part of social science and, in the spirit of Weber's ideal types (Weber 1968: 19–22), the themes here constitute an ideal type which never exactly conform to any one case, but which aid our understanding of the particularities of any one case by reference to generality. They are useful, then, in both guiding us through the specifics of any particular case and helping us gain a general understanding of populism.

At its root, populism, as a set of ideas, has a fundamental ambivalence about politics, especially representative politics. Politics is messy and corrupting, and involvement comes only under extreme circumstances. In this sense, populism seeks to avoid habitual political involvement. Populism is reluctantly political. Overcoming their reluctance, populists engage in politics when they perceive crises. The way populists are eventually political also gives expression to their ambivalence. Eschewing the complexity of representative politics, populists advocate simplicity and directness in their politics. The accoutrements of representative politics, including parties and parliaments, are all too often, for populists, distractions and unnecessary complications. It is a profound dilemma for populism that while representative politics is treated with hostility, it is only under such a form of politics that populism finds systematic expression and the possibility of mobilization as a political force.

While populism is a negative reaction to representative politics, it does have a more positive side. Populism tends to identify itself with an idealized version of its chosen people, and to locate them in a similarly idealized landscape. In doing this, populism excludes elements it sees as alien, corrupt or debased, and works on a distinction between the things which are wholesome and those which are not, between what I shall term the 'heartland' and the margins. Populism therefore has implicit within it a conception of a heartland. This is a notion that is constructed through looking inward and backward: a world that embodies the collective ways and wisdom of the people who construct it, usually with reference to what has gone before (even if that is idealized). The heartland is populated by 'the people' and gives meaning to constructions and invocations of the people by populists. Some suggest that a commitment to 'the people' is what defines populism. This is problematic because 'the people' means fundamentally different things to different populists (Canovan 1984). It is much more fruitful to recognize that the commitment to 'the people' is a concept that is derived from a sense of a heartland.

Populism has been a tool of progressives, of reactionaries, of democrats, of autocrats, of the left and of the right. The reason for its adaptability lies in the 'empty heart' of populism: populism lacks a commitment to key values. While other ideologies contain, either implicitly or explicitly, a focus on one or more values such as equality, liberty and social justice, populism has no such core to it. This explains why populism is appropriated by such a wide range of political positions. It also explains why populism is very often appended to other ideologies. Populism's natural position is as an adjective attached to other ideas that fill the space at the empty heart of populism. The 'grand' ideologies of the modern age – liberalism, conservatism, feminism and socialism – are likely to have adjectives attached to them to make them into social liberalism or radical feminism. Populism is more likely to attach itself than be attached to.

The emergence of a crisis shakes populists out of their reluctance and into politics, and into an active defence of the heartland. The difficulty is that the crisis may be one in the imagination of the populist or it may be an economic and political crisis in the true sense of the word (i.e. a situation that cannot, by definition, be sustained). I do not want to make the judgment about whether the crises are real or imaginary, so it is easier, and perhaps more accurate, to observe that populism comes about when a larger process of transition gives rise to a sense of crisis, at least among one social group.

Populism's ambivalence about politics helps to explain why it is so often an episodic phenomenon. Eschewing the institutions, forms and patterns of representative politics, populism deliberately tries to translate the simplicity and plain-talking of ordinary people into structures that are simple and direct. Locking on to leaders or bypassing parties altogether, however, has its problems, and these mean that populism is invariably a passing phenomenon. It limits itself because of its attitude towards institutions.

Populism has an essentially chameleonic quality that means it always takes on the hue of the environment in which it occurs. This is not as a disguise or camouflage, because populism is *always* partially constituted by aspects of the environment in which it finds itself. Another way of saying this is to say that populism has primary and secondary features, and that one of its primary features is that it takes on, as a matter of course, secondary features from its context. All ideologies do this to an extent, but populism constructs narratives, myths and symbols that, because they must resonate with the heartland, draw on the surroundings to a fundamental degree.

In summarizing the themes, it is possible to suggest that populism is a reaction against the ideas, institutions and practices of representative politics which celebrates an implicit or explicit heartland as a response to a sense of crisis; however, lacking universal key values, it is chameleonic, taking on attributes of its environment, and, in practice, is episodic. Populism is an episodic, anti-political, empty-hearted, chameleonic celebration of the heartland in the face of crisis.

Populism appears not only in many different places and times but also in different forms. As an epithet, 'populist' has been fitted to movements, leaders, regimes, ideas and styles. The popularity of populism as a term attaches disproportionately to the last, but least, of these. To say that things are done in a 'populist' manner is not to tell us much about the politics of populism. If they are done in a populist way because they embody a deeper commitment to populist ideas, then it is on the populist ideas that we should focus (cf. Richards 1981). Often populist style is confused with a style that simply seeks to be popular – to appeal to a wide range of people. This is not simply an incomplete but also an inaccurate use of the term.

Populist movements and parties, politicians, regimes and ideas are the focus of this book because looking at them unlocks the key to understanding the politics of populism.[1] Culturally, populism runs through societies as a celebration of the virtue of ordinary people and often as romanticized visions of the lifestyles and landscapes, but I am concerned here with populism once it is a political phenomenon, when it is mobilized. In this sense, populist movements and parties (whether created from the bottom up or from above by leaders) underlie all the other manifestations. Populist leaders create movements and parties to legitimate them. Populist ideas are only political in so far as they are taken up by movements and parties. Regimes rely on leaders and, in turn on the parties and movements that legitimate them.

Looking at what populism can be demonstrates that it is rarely just a movement, leader, regime or idea. Usually it is a combination, but notably it is never all of these at the same time. In the case of the US Populist movement at the close of the nineteenth century, we have a genuinely popular movement with a developed and complex set of populist ideas, but we also have a movement that never made it into government and so never became a regime, and we have a movement that was not tied to any one particular leader. In contrast, the Latin American experience of populism has been the opposite, in that it encompasses the regimes of particular figures (such as Juan Perón in Argentina) whose leadership was more important than the construction of a populist set of ideas or of a populist movement. In the case of the Russian *narodniki* at the end of the nineteenth century, there was the attempt to spread a set of ideas through the leadership of the educated and the hope of creating a popular movement, but again a failure to take the reins of power. With political figures in the politics of the United States, such as Huey Long in Louisiana and George Wallace in Alabama, we have leaders with populist ideas but without movements. In these two cases it is valid to talk in terms of regimes as these men implemented, as much as they could, populist policies. We have, in populism, a variety of not only manifestations but also a variety of forms in which these manifestations occur.

Looking at examples of populism in history can be frustrating. If we seek to use populism to explain politics in any one case, we invariably end up somewhat irked by the awkward shape of the concept of populism. Inevitably, in the light of expert and specific knowledge, the concept is taken, slightly reshaped, refashioned and polished so that its sheen reflects much better the specifics of the example to hand. The concept becomes therefore a better reflection of the context but less faithful to the idea of a universal concept of populism. In its newly fashioned shape it can even become an integral part of the way we explain politics in the context. But as soon as we examine the way it has been similarly reshaped and refashioned to explain politics elsewhere, the resemblance seems limited.

Each case of populism tends to lead to emphasis on one of the factors present as the definitive feature of populism. Looking at the Russian case, it is tempting to see the peasantry and the romanticization of peasant life as the key to populism. But looking at nineteenth-century populism in the United States, our attention is far more likely to be on agrarian radicalism that has little in common with the romantic view of the Russian peasant. Moving south, Latin American populism shifts out of the countryside to become a movement for the urban working classes. Populism in Canada has drawn on farmers and on agricultural workers. And coming to Europe, the new populism of the far right becomes fundamentally urban and exclusionary. Moving round the globe and through history does not move us, in itself, closer to the essence of populism.

If we try and take a more generalist approach and use a range of examples to illustrate the concept, we face another irksome fact. None of the examples illustrates all of the facets of populism. Some come close (notably the example of the US Populists in the nineteenth century) but none go all the way. Populism, as an empirical phenomenon, is an uncomfortable composite of historical and contemporary cases. This has led some to reject the search for its essence and to instead content themselves with dividing it up into different types (among them Canovan, 1981, 1982). In the following pages, I attempt to show that it is worth attempting an ideal type of populism through examining specific populist movements, parties, ideas and regimes.

In Part One I offer a survey of the history of populism as it has appeared in different cases. This part provides the empirical material around which the conceptual discussions of the rest of the book are built. The selection of cases is not easy. There are many other examples that can be characterized as populist but which I have not included, but I have attempted to bring to the fore the major examples of populism. My purpose in providing five chapters describing various populisms is to provide a brief introduction to those histories without which we cannot have a full understanding of populism. In the process I draw out elements of populism.

In Chapter 2, I survey the various definitions of populism that already exist and suggest that we should differentiate between three approaches to populism as a concept. First, and most commonly, *contextual* definitions are confined to one particular example of populism. Second, *variegated* definitions deny that there is a universal essence of populism and seek to construct taxonomies of different populisms. Third, as I am attempting to suggest in this book, there is the attempt to build a genuinely *universal* understanding of populism.

Those readers looking for comprehensiveness in the cases I focus on will not find it. Those readers looking for particular exclusions may well find them.[2] The main emphasis I have taken is on North America, Russia, Latin America and Western Europe. The choice of these is for a number of reasons. First, the cases represent as near to a 'canon' of populisms as we have. In other words, these are the cases that are most usually used when we talk of populism. Second, these cases separately highlight key features of populism and

collectively constitute a minimally sufficient set for understanding
it. The North American cases exemplify a mass movement of populism. The Russian case highlights a rural romanticization of a heartland. The Latin American cases show us the importance and
problems of populist leadership and regimes. Finally, the Western
European cases bring out powerfully the anti-institutional element
of populism.

Another reason for these cases is that many of the individuals
concerned either explicitly call themselves populist or do not demur
from that description imposed on them by others. This is important to note because populism's deeply embedded hostility towards
elites and intellectuals means that self-describing themselves with
a term that has great stigma for elites and intellectuals shows them
to be populist, at least instinctively. It is a necessary part of being a
populist to not see the label as negative.

There is a particular need in analysing populism to do so with
the benefit of knowledge about many of its historical manifestations. The lack of a consensus about what populism is means that
historical case studies give a necessary grounding that would
otherwise be lacking. The fact that populism is episodic rather
than omnipresent means that it is easier mentally to handle the
important cases as there are not too many of them. Another
reason for surveying populism is less practical and more theo-
logical. The chameleonic quality of populism allows us to use
populism to illuminate the context in which it finds itself, but it
also means that to understand populism in its wider sense we need
to be aware of what are its environmental and what are its essential features.

The fate of populism as a concept and an object of study mirrors
the history of populism itself. Populism has been studied episodi-
cally, coming in surges. This no doubt owes much to intellectual
fashionableness but interestingly does not follow regularly from
particular upsurges in populism as we might expect. The debate
also is a very fractured one. Putting the pieces together is necessarily an unsatisfactory process because the different pieces have
been fashioned for separate and distinct environments. It is crucial,
if we want to understand representative politics and political ideologies, that we must be prepared to engage in this process. It is
only if we have some understanding of populism that we can have
a full understanding of representative politics.

Notes

1 For those who study culture and communication, the term 'populism' has been heavily used and has become central to the field of cultural studies. In this sense, it is used very specifically and has little in common with more political uses of the term which are the focus here. Cultural populism describes a position which privileges the culture that is consumed by ordinary people, rather than the 'high' culture as consumed by elites (McGuigan 1992: 1–5).
2 For a comprehensive overview, it is impossible to do better than refer to Canovan (1981).

2
Definitions of Populism

Populism serves many masters and mistresses. At different times and in different places it has been a force for change, a force against change, a creature of progressive politics of the left, the refuge of a measured defence of the status quo and a companion of the extreme right. Populists have been portrayed as dupes, democrats and demons. The term is used widely, but often defined narrowly. It is used to dismiss some proposal as too popular, or as popular with certain sorts of people (invariably the wrong sort). Attempts to identify a core of populism – something that runs through it in all its various guises – have left some writers with the clear sense that there is no clear sense to it (for example, Mouzelis 1985: 344; Taguieff 1995: 17, 25).

For such a commonly used term, it is surprising how little attention populism has received as a concept. Where it has been dealt with systematically, populism as a concept has found little agreement surrounding it. Like the emergence of populist movements themselves, attempts to capture the essence of populism have sprung up at different times and in different places, but it is very difficult to see a consistent pattern. Most have seen populism as specific to the context in which they are focused. The more ambitious have attempted to define populism in universal terms. Others have portrayed it as variegated – with no essence but with varieties.

The difference between contextual, universal and variegated approaches to defining populism is due, in part, to the different types of work that deal with populism. By definition, historical studies of particular manifestations of populism are contextual. Many contextual definitions of populism – including agrarian radicalism, Peronism, ideas of Social Credit and *narodnichestvo* – come from the detailed study of one context. It is in the nature of a detailed and single-focus historical study that the larger implications may remain implicit. If there has been an explicit attempt at definition, even if it is contextual, then it is potentially generalizable if those implications are made explicit and systematically applied. We can always potentially develop our understanding of the concept by attempting to apply one contextual definition to another context. If we do this we find very quickly that many contextual definitions do not travel well, that the concept of populism (as opposed to its particular manifestation) is framed in terms that are too specific. On the other hand there are some studies of populism which are contextually derived and which make no attempt to be universal but which have developed conceptualizations of populism that travel far better.

In this chapter I address those studies which have explicitly attempted to generalize about populism (universalistic or variegated) or which are explicitly contextual but implicitly generalizable, to offer a survey of the 'state of the art' for students of populism.

The state of the art

Edward Shils gave a contextual definition of populism when he wrote in direct reaction to the McCarthyism of the United States in the 1950s. Seeing populism as multifaceted and as permeating Nazi dictatorship in Germany and Bolshevism in Russian, Shils suggests that populism 'exists wherever there is an ideology of popular resentment against the order imposed on society by a long-established, differentiated ruling class which is believed to have a monopoly of power, property, breeding and culture' (Shils 1956: 100–1). For Shils the key to understanding populism lies in the relationship between elites and masses. Populism is portrayed as deeply ambivalent in its attitude towards institutions – those of the state, universities, bureaucracy, financial institutions. Unsurprisingly, populism therefore fundamentally distrusts those peopling those institutions as not only corrupt but also as lacking in wisdom. Wisdom resides in the people and, in so far as political institutions identify with – not represent – the will of the people, politics is seen as legitimate (Shils 1956: 101–3).

The phenomenon of McCarthyism during the 1950s had an important effect on the academic debate about populism in the

USA, alarming many as to the dangerous possibilities of extremism. It was in this context that Shils was writing. After McCarthy
there were a number of studies that sought to explore and explain
the outburst of right-wing extremism in the USA (Lipset 1963; Bell
1963; Rogin 1967; Lipset and Raab 1971). Two orientations guided
this set of writings. The first was that a lineage was traced between
the People's Party and the ideas of the populist movement in that
era and McCarthyism. Consequently, the previous populism was
very much portrayed as being extremist, bigoted and backward.
The second orientation of these studies was therefore a desire to
establish the social bases of support for populism, to see if there was
something particular about the type of people who had been drawn
to this form of extremism.

Shils later extended his analysis of populism to explain populism
in Africa and Asia. He did so in an explicitly comparative fashion
and suggests that populism results from the emergence of a global
intellectual community and is therefore 'a phenomenon of the
tension between metropolis and province which arises from the
trend toward that world-wide intellectual community' (Shils 1962:
214). Drawing on the history of populism, he sees its roots as lying
in German history with the rejection and critique of the rule of the
state, the universities and the church authorities. In its place there
was the belief in the 'folk' or the people. Drawing the parallels with
populism in the USA and Russia to describe the populism of the
intellectual elites in African and Asia, Shils argues that populism is
characterized by oppositionalism.

Kornhauser drew on Shils's definition of populism for his own
analysis of mass society. He argued that populism is both cause and
effect in mass society, as it is the denial of plurality and the assertion of uniformity in the face of social differentiation (Kornhauser
1959: 103). Mass society therefore gives rise to populist democracy,
which he contrasted to liberal democracy. Populist democracy
involves direct participation of the people as a way of circumvent-
ing the institutions and associations of representation and also has
the effect of taking away the liberty of the individual as the people,
assumed to be monolithic, have the priority (Kornhauser 1959:
131–2).

Shils places a stress on the new conditions of a world-wide intellectual community and the knock-on effect this has on the relationship between elites and (particular) sections of society in particular
national contexts. This reflects an underlying continuity in many

definitions of populism, that it is a reaction to modernity or to a particular feature of the modern world. And, although Shils's initial concern was with the USA, this focus on the twin strains of domestic relations between rulers and ruled, combined with relations between core and periphery in a more global setting, is one that has a natural resonance for those studying those parts of the world that find themselves on the economic periphery.

Torcuato Di Tella examines populism in Latin America but does so in a way that is explicitly comparative, especially with the European experience. In his earlier work on populism, Di Tella attempted to draw out different types of populism that occurred in Latin America as an illustration of how Latin American development was different from European development (Di Tella 1965). With the 1989 revolutions in Europe, Di Tella began to draw parallels between the Latin American experience and Eastern Europe (Di Tella 1997). Explicitly, Di Tella stresses that populism comes when there is an anti-status-quo motivation among middle-level elites, when rising expectations creates a mobilized mass of citizens and when the conditions allow collective enthusiasm among elites and masses (Di Tella 1965: 53). He defines it as 'a political movement based on a mobilized but not yet autonomously organized popular sector, led by an elite rooted among the middle and upper echelons of society, and kept together by a charismatic, personalized link between leader and led' (Di Tella 1997: 196). He argues that populism emerges in these conditions where social democratic parties would emerge in economically more developed countries (Di Tella 1965, 1997). Populism is therefore, for Di Tella, a function of the process of development of societies as they move towards modernity.

Implicitly, Di Tella stresses that populism is characterized by a sense of differentiation between those who are poor and those who are part of the elite and by the social characteristics of the supporting coalition. The sense of differentiation is important, but the attempt to characterize populism by the social make-up of populist movements inevitably limits the scope of populism because it has had some very different social bases in its various manifestations.

Di Tella emphasizes that a sense of differentiation occurs both between elites in less economically developed countries who compare themselves with elites in more developed countries, and between social groups and their sense of grievance at the status quo. These social groups are both the educated who feel that they are unable to satisfy their aspirations and the uneducated mass whose low social status and poor living conditions foster a sense of grievance (Di Tella 1965: 52).

The difficulty of Di Tella's account of populism is that it assumes that societies find themselves on or move themselves along a fixed continuum of development. Implicit in it is the assumption of a single goal of modern development. This does not allow for fundamental variations that occur in both the nature of development and in the end point of societies. The second problem is that populism occurs in societies in which economies and societies are, in these terms, definitively modern. It is possible to see the USA as an almost paradigmatic example of populism (Kazin 1995). Populism is a recurrent feature in European politics. It is nonetheless a recurring characteristic of those who have come to the concept of populism from an interest in the Third World or Latin America, like Di Tella, to see it as a feature of societies at a particular stage of development (see also, for example, Malloy 1977; Germani 1978).

Many of the themes developed by writers focusing on the Latin American experience have had resonance for those studying politics in Africa and the Third World in general. Gavin Kitching places populism at the centre of his analysis of thinking about development. He argues that populism is a reaction to industrialization and is characterized by a championing of small-scale production and opposed to concentration of production (Kitching 1989: 19–22). It is therefore a heavily economistic analysis and particularly focused around peasant ideologies, and therefore he draws heavily on the Russian populists as the paradigmatic example of this sort of thinking.

The difficulty of Kitching's account of populism is that it is too specific. The concept of populism is developed to trace a continuity within a strand of thinking about political economy. The problem is not that this is imprecise, but that Kitching derives populism from what is developed and not from the impulse that causes this sort of thinking to develop. Populism is essentially a reaction to rule. In the context of agrarian peasant societies, this reaction will, if given political expression, crystallize into a set of ideas. However, it is in the reaction and not the development of that reaction that we find the essence of populism. Looking at Perón's populism, the concepts and ideas he developed had an essentially pliant quality, and this is testament to the impulse that gives rise to them. Kitching gives priority to the secondary characteristics of populism.

All populisms develop additional ideas, but these are not the ideas that make them populist.

Ghiţa Ionescu and Ernest Gellner, in organizing a conference at the London School of Economics in 1967, tried to bring together experts in the different manifestations of populism in order to draw out a more general theory. The conference involved 43 participants and the range of geographical areas covered was extremely wide and therefore potentially avoided the specificity of other attempts to theorize populism.

In the introduction to the book which came out of the conference and which remains *the* definitive collection on populism (Ionescu and Gellner 1969a), the editors say that it is an 'attempt to clarify the main aspects of a concept which during the nineteenth century and even more in the twentieth century has been more fundamental to the shaping of the political mind than is generally acknowledged' (Ionescu and Gellner 1969b: 5). They explicitly tackle the questions that need to be answered if populism is to be identified as a unified phenomenon. They ask whether populism can be considered an ideology, a recurring mentality brought about by similar conditions, a political psychology, an anti phenomenon (anti-capitalist, anti-urban, anti-Semitic), a pro-people phenomenon, or as a mentality absorbed by socialism, nationalism and peasantism (Ionescu and Gellner 1969b: 3–4). Despite their hopes, the resulting collection does not identify a core set of ideas common to populism, although it remains collectively a landmark study and does yield some important individual contributions.

In his chapter in the collection, Peter Worsley explicitly surveys populism in the USA, Russia, Africa, Asia and Latin America but comes to the conclusion that the only common aspects are of a high level of generality (by implication, of limited use) and that therefore populism 'is better regarded as an emphasis, a dimension of political culture in general, not simply as a particular kind of overall ideological system or type of organization' (Worsley 1969: 245). He returns to Shils's definition which stresses the importance of popular sovereignty and of direct contact between government and the people as the nearest his survey leads him to a common core (Worsely 1969: 243–6).

Confining himself to a 'Third World' variant of populism, Worsley is less general and suggests that it is characterized by four features. First, that societies are portrayed as essentially homogeneous, with only non-antagonistic divisions within them. This means that politics is classless and that the indigenous society is 'natural', constituting a community. Second, the real conflict comes between the society or nation and the external world, especially colonial powers. Third, the community is expressed through one dominant party that fuses the ideas of community, society and nation. Fourth, the party becomes an agent of liberation and a force for economic development (Worsley 1969: 229–30, 1967: 165–7).

Emboldened by 'a lack of specialist knowledge', Peter Wiles outlines 24 features of populism as a syndrome (Wiles 1969). Populism is moralistic; of a certain style of appearance; dependent on extraordinary leaders; as an ill-disciplined movement, self-consciously loose in its self-definition; anti-intellectuals; anti-establishment; capable of ineffective and short-winded violence; class-conscious but conciliatory, avoiding class war; corrupted and bourgeosified by success; given to small-scale cooperation; supported by those of limited wealth; vigorously opposed to financiers; potentially less critical of large-scale productive capitalists; possibly urban (as well as rural); supportive of state intervention; opposed to social and economic inequality caused by institutions it opposes; in foreign policy particularly suspicious of the military establishment but isolationist in orientation; for religion but against the religious establishment; disdainful of science and technology; nostalgic; mildly racialist to a great extent; various (spanning pre-industrial, peasant anti-industrialism, farmer industry-tolerating); and not to be thought of as bad (Wiles 1969: 167–71).

In his attempt to sum up the overall sense of the discussion at the conference, Isaiah Berlin proposed that there was general agreement over six features of populism that applied across the different variants. The first feature is commitment to *Gemeinschaft* (approximately community), which gives rise to the idea of an integrated and coherent society. The second feature is that populism is apolitical in the sense that it is not interested in political institutions because it believes in society before it believes in the state. Populism is concerned with returning people to their natural and spontaneous condition to which they belonged before having been subject to some sort of spiritual collapse. The fourth element is that populism is past-directed, in the sense that it seeks to bring back ancient values in to the contemporary world. Berlin 'tentatively' adds to this list that populism, although referring to different versions of the people, always seeks to speak in the name of the majority. Finally, he suggests that populism emerges in societies undergoing or about to undergo modernization (Berlin *et al.* 1968: 173–8).

Ernesto Laclau (1977) puts forward a theory of populism which forcefully takes on its apparently contradictory and elusive nature, and which embodies a commitment to a Marxist account. He suggests that the attempt to generalize about populism, by working out what are the common features for a series of movements described as populist, is circular. To focus on the movements as populist means already knowing what populism amounts to. The outcome is to generalize about a series of movements that are essentially different (Laclau 1977: 145). Laclau starts his analysis of populism from the point that populism is fundamentally elusive as a concept and apparently contradictory. Laclau accounts for this in a complex way. He argues that the dominant ideas of a society, those that represent the thinking of the dominant or hegemonic class, will always, as an expression of their dominance, absorb other ideas and neutralize them by allowing their expression but only in a way that projects them as different but not as fundamentally antagonistic. In one sense, therefore, populism can be seen as the ideology of elites. This occurs when one fraction of the dominant class seeks to establish hegemony but is unable to do so and so makes a direct appeal to the masses (Laclau 1977: 173).

For Laclau, society must be accounted for in terms of contradiction between social forces that reflect partially the contradictions in the process of production. In simplified form, societies express class antagonisms. However, he sees that sometimes there is a wider conflict that does not accord with particular classes – the popular traditions of a society will reflect the wider concerns of popular masses who are not part of the dominant class and who are the subjects of rule. This is the conflict between the 'people' and the 'power bloc'. Ideas that call on the dominated classes in this respect are called popular-democratic ideas. When particular class antagonisms are expressed in popular-democratic forms, then populism occurs but it necessarily has, for Laclau, both a class form and a popular-democratic form. Put more simply, it speaks simultaneously for a class and for the 'people', even though they are not the same thing. This feature explains why populism is so elusive because conflict between 'people' and 'power bloc' is so pervasive and yet so different in its manifestations. Part of that difference will lie in the classes that mobilize against the 'power bloc', and this explains why populism has historically been attached to such a range of classes.

Margaret Canovan (1981) offers the most ambitious attempts to get to grips with populism. Her work gives a variegated approach differentiating between agrarian populism and political populism. This covers the range of populist movements throughout history and across the world. Detailed consideration of these means that she breaks down agrarian populism into the populism of farmers, of peasants and of intellectuals. Comparing the rural radicalism of the US People's Party, the Canadian Social Credit movement in the 1930s and the German agrarian movement of the 1890s, she rejects the temptation to describe them as *sui generis* phenomena and traces lines of continuity. Those lines come, for her, in the demands of farmers for government intervention in the economy (Canovan 1981: 104).

Moving to the rural radicalism of the Russian *narodnichestvo*, and comparing this with Algerian, Tanzanian and Bolivian forms of agrarian socialism, Canovan draws out the common tendency for these forms of populism to oscillate between idealized deference for the peasantry and the need to provide leadership for this idealized group (Canovan 1981: 109). In these cases, she suggests that the role of elites in attempting to catalyse and mobilize the rural population means that this form of agrarian populism is effectively that of the intellectuals. It takes what Canovan describes as a different form of agrarian populism for the peasantry to unequivocally take centre stage. It is in the peasant parties of Eastern Europe which emerged in the early twentieth century and which grew into the Green Uprising that Canovan sees the peasant variant of agrarian populism. This movement in Poland, Romania, Bulgaria and Czechoslovakia after the First World War attempted to develop and implement ideas of voluntary cooperation between peasants with an emphasis on democracy, family property and an antagonism to the cities. Canovan suggests that there is enough overlap between these different types of agrarian populism to 'make intelligible the use of a single term' but not 'to unite all these movements into a single political phenomenon with a single ideology, program, or socioeconomic base' (Canovan 1981: 133).

An exclusive focus on agrarian populism misses much. As Canovan (1981: 136) suggests, it is therefore important to consider those parts of populism that are 'political'. She suggests that it needs to incorporate populist dictatorship, populist democracy, reactionary populism and politicians' populism. As soon as we consider Latin American examples of populism, it becomes clear that it cannot be considered as exclusively agrarian as they were urban movements with strong leaders invoking the wider 'people' (in practice a combination of the urban working class and the peasantry) in the name of reformist programmes. Moving north, Canovan brings into the same fold the politics of Huey Long, governor of Louisiana between 1928 and 1932 and US senator between 1932 and 1935. Long's appeal was based on his denunciation of the concentration of wealth in Wall Street, on his programmes of social improvement for Louisiana, but achieved through Machiavellian and strong-arm politics of deception. Like Perón, Long was a strong leader of the poor but there was nothing necessarily agrarian about his politics.

The second sense in which Canovan uses the term 'political populism' is to describe those sets of institutions that are associated with the practices of direct democracy. Out of the populist movement of the nineteenth century in the USA came the roots of what was the Progressive movement in the early twentieth century. Unlike the Populist movement and the People's Party, this movement was largely driven by ideas from above rather than being a genuinely mass movement. Like the populist movement, it distrusted the institutions of representative politics and sought to introduce mechanisms that bypassed the role of representatives through mechanisms such as the initiative, the referendum and the recall. Moves to supplement the US model of democracy with these institutions worked best in the West where they were building on the roots laid by nineteenth-century populism (Canovan 1981: 177). Implicit in the need to supplement democracy with these institutions is the assumption that representative democracy can over-represent certain interests and that its institutions can become captured by powerful interests, so transforming benign representative institutions into levers of power for the already powerful. Canovan makes the comparison with Switzerland where the institutions of direct democracy are not so much additional institutional features, but rather integral parts of the governmental structure. The Swiss case illustrates that populist forms of democracy can yield a system which stresses decentralization and the extensive use of referendums to overcome a highly fragmented and segmented population and which produces a form of functioning democracy in difficult circumstances, and provides us with a model with which to assess the 'virtues and defects of populist democracy' (Canovan 1981: 202).

The third form of political populism that Canovan suggests is that of reactionary populism. Canovan compares the case of George Wallace in the US state of Alabama with Enoch Powell in Britain. In 1968 Wallace, building on his record of protest against racial desegregation, stood as a third party candidate for the presidency while, in the same year, Powell made a speech in which he warned against the dangers of immigration for British culture. Both were united in making appeals that stressed the gap between the values of elites and those of the people, revealing 'a clash between reactionary, authoritarian, racist, or chauvinist views at the grass roots, and the progressive, liberal, tolerant cosmopolitan characteristic of the elite' (Canovan 1981: 229). What also united both politicians was that they were reacting against the apparent tide of progress. Canovan makes the point that this clash between progress and populism is heavily dependent on the context, on what is seen as 'progress'. In this sense populism, as a reaction to the prevailing dominant ideas, can be both reactive and yet rational. What is, in Canovan's terms, 'disreputable' can also be a reaction on the part of popular opinion to real conditions of hardship (Canovan 1981: 257–8).

The final type of political populism for Canovan is politicians' populism. This is a style of politics that plays on the ambiguity on who 'the people' are. In considering accounts of populism drawing on African experiences, it is clear that there are claims by some politicians to represent a unified people above and beyond divisions that otherwise cross their country. These are used to justify systems of one-party rule. In another sense, politicians also try and construct a unified people through creating cross-class or 'catch-all' coalitions. Jimmy Carter's successful campaign for the US presidency saw him using the populist imagery of the outsider, the honest farmer seeking office, while at the same time deliberately appealing to both liberal and conservative instincts in the electorate (Canovan 1981: 269–73).

Canovan, in outlining her seven categories, makes the point that no core to populism can be found, but rather we can identify a number of different syndromes. Bringing out the similarities across the seven types allows her to suggest that there are clusters of similarities around the 'populism of the little man', authoritarian populism and revolutionary populism (Canovan 1981: 291–2). She also suggests that particular historical manifestations of populism can both combine and separate the categories (Canovan 1981: 293). The only common themes across all seven types are a resort to appeals to the people and a distrust of elites (Canovan 1981: 264), and the usefulness of this is limited at best (Canovan 1981: 298). Her conclusion is that populism is a term that is widely used and so it is important to provide some clarity, but that it incorporates a wide range of phenomena without a common core, and that there-fore her attempt to provide a taxonomy is the only way to deal with this complexity.

A more recent attempt to theorize populism as a concept has come from the radical (and frequently iconoclastic) US journal of critical social theory, *Telos*. Although contributors have varied in their positions, it is possible to see a clear project of attempting to formulate populism as a concept, to fashion it as a tool for the development of the sort of critical theory with which the journal is associated. The core of the *Telos* position is that populism offers the best hope for a critique of, and alternative to, the hegemony of liberalism. The need for this alternative is heightened by the present crisis of 'New Deal' liberalism as exemplified in US society and politics, and by the disjunction between the 'New Class' of well-educated, professionalized, bureaucratized elites who have devel-oped from the need to steer the technocratic tools of the new regulatory state and the traditional middle- and working-class support base for the New Deal politics. The *Telos* position shares my emphasis on populism as a reaction to liberalism (to the insti-tutions of liberal democratic politics in my case). Specifically focus-ing on the misfit between elites in representative politics and the communities that give rise to them, *Telos* argues for the need to reinvigorate local politics and responsible individual participation in that politics, thus seeing populism as a potentially liberatory political project.

Taking the rise of the regional leagues (such as the Lega Nord) in Italy as an indicator of the broader applicability of their thesis, the journal has attempted to develop populism as the new route for critical theory's critique of liberalism, combining it with a radical democratic position. *Telos* has seen the possibility of the degener-ation of populism into racism and a new exclusionary ideology, but views this as a potential danger rather than either essential to or inevitable in populism. Despite the attempt to examine the popu-list possibilities in Europe, it remains clear that the *Telos* concept of populism, although well theorized, is really embedded in the US context. The importance of the particular constellation of liberalism in US political institutions ('New Deal liberalism'), as well as the explicit reference to the founding ideas of US democracy (see Piccone 1995), means that the *Telos* concept of populism is specific in both time and place to the United States in the post-Reagan era.

Surveying the state of the art on the conceptualization of populism *qua* populism brings out four clear features. The first is the relatively small amount of material dealing with populism as a concept. This is all the more surprising given the wide and popular use of the term. The second feature is that those conceptualizations that have attempted to be either conceptually bold or explicitly comparative have almost invariably carried the imprint of the contexts in which they were originally developed, and are therefore too narrow to help us develop a more universalistic conceptualization. The third feature is that the most explicit attempt to draw out a conceptualization by aggregating studies from an almost global span of case studies (Ionescu and Gellner 1969a) failed to deliver a synthesis of what was clearly an unparalleled range of scholarship and expertise. The final feature is that, in Canovan's (1981) work, the attempt to be both broad in scope and bold in conceptualization led to a conclusion that populism is essentially a fractured concept.

Note

1 For various articles and collections of articles representing the *Telos* position, see Anderson *et al.* 1991; *Telos* 1991, 1991–92, 1995a, 1995b; Piccone 1991. See also Lasch 1991.

Cases of Populism

3

The Politics of Movements and Populist Politics in the United States of America

It is hard to understand politics in the United States without having some sense of populism. It is impossible to understand populism without having a sense of the populism in the USA. The construction of the political system, as embodied in the Constitution, and of the very national identity of the USA has been around principles of representative democracy. Populism therefore, as a reaction to representative politics, runs through US politics like a motif.

The People's Party and the Populist movement that gave rise to it in the late nineteenth century loom large in the populist pantheon. The story looms less prominently in the political history of the United States. Failure to break through as an independent and new force into the US party system means that, in retrospect, the Populists are often in danger of being squeezed between the trauma of the Civil War in the 1860s and Roosevelt's realigning New Deal in the 1930s, as an interesting but inconsequential historical diversion from the gladiatorial conflict between the two persistent

parties, Democratic and Republican, in US politics. The importance of the People's Party and the Populist movement in the 1880s
and 1890s is much more than this. They embodied, articulated and
mobilized embedded populist motifs that run deeply through US
politics.

Looking out from the USA, the history of the People's Party
offers populism its clearest case of the mobilization of a mass movement from underneath. The nature of nineteenth-century US populism was not a function of particular charismatic leaders (as in the
case of Perón), or of studied groups of elites and theorists developing and then implementing complex abstract ideological frame-
works (as in the Russian case). The People's Party bore the imprint
of the movement, a popular mass movement, that gave rise to it. In
the history of the People's Party, more than in any of the other cases
of populism we are considering, we have the politics of a mass
movement, of a truly bottom-up phenomenon. Taking the 'people'
in name was also indicative of the really popular nature of the
movement among farmers in the South and West. The US Populist
movement and People's Party demonstrate the possibility of a progressive populism: one that moves towards radical change but short
of revolution.

Populism in the USA does not start and end with the People's
Party. As Michael Kazin (1995) argues, populism is essential to US
politics. Kazin suggests that its roots lie deeply embedded in a
combination of anti-elitism and nineteenth-century ideas eman-
ating from the Protestant reformation and the Enlightenment,
specifically 'pietism' and rationalism, that came to be woven
together into the fabric of meaning that underlies 'Americanism'.
The key for Kazin is that this 'persistent yet mutable style of political rhetoric' (Kazin 1995: 5) can be transformed from progressive,
reformist left-wing ideology to conservative and reactionary ideology, as indeed it has been. In all these guises it can claim the ardour
and fervour of a reformist movement without ever veering over the
line into revolutionary thought. Populism, for Kazin, allows US
politics to see apparent challenges but without ever threatening the
fundamental ideological structure of US politics.

Kazin draws out the populist lineage starting with the People's
Party but running through the demands of labour in the early
part of the twentieth century, with its opposition to the centralized
state and concentration of corporate wealth. In the temperance
movement, which succeeded in attaining Prohibition, Kazin sees

populism in the claims that moneyed interests were keeping the poor drunk and incapable of protest. With the politics of Father Frank Coughlin and his attempt to construct a new force against the corporate moguls and communist revolutions, Kazin sees a populism that was initially in keeping with Franklin Delano Roosevelt's attacks on 'economic royalists' but which ended up at odds with Americanism through Coughlan's support for the fascists in the Second World War.

It is in the Cold War that Kazin suggests that the populist turn from progressive politics to conservative politics of reaction takes place. Through the anti-communist witch-hunt of McCarthy in the very portals of Congress and in the politics of race through George Wallace in the South, the scene was set for the final capture of populism by the right in the politics of Richard Nixon and Ronald Reagan.

There is a danger with a tightly focused lens that detail comes into sharper relief than the larger contours of the surrounding area. Looking for populism in all corners of US politics, it is not difficult to find either the clear shapes or shadows of populism almost everywhere. Looking more widely at populism, it is clear that it has a particular resonance in US politics but that real movements of populism as significant moments, movements or movers in US politics are less numerous than Kazin's approach would suggest. Kazin is looking at populism through the lens of US politics, but looking at US politics through the lens of populism means that the picture is somewhat different.

The People's Party and the Populist movement

In Omaha in 1892, a national convention of the newly formed People's Party met to nominate a candidate for the presidential election. From a background of grass-roots regional movements of farmers creating cooperatives and alliances to offset their reliance on the Eastern banking and railroad establishments had emerged a fully-fledged party. The move into party politics had by no means been a foregone conclusion for a movement of agrarian radicals. It marked an important change in focus for the populists. The party they created was unsuccessful. It could not breach the two-party dominance of the Democrats and Republicans. But the story of the People's Party and the nineteenth-century US populists is a vital key to understanding populism generally. At Omaha, the party adopted a platform as well as a candidate. In the preamble to the platform, based on an impassioned speech by Ignatius Donnelly, we find a classic statement of populist principles:

> [W]e meet in the midst of a nation brought to the verge of moral, political, and material ruin. Corruption dominates the ballot-box, the Legislatures, the Congress, and touches even the ermine of the bench. The people are demoralized . . . The newspapers are largely subsidized or muzzled, public opinion silenced, business prostrated, homes covered with mortgages, labor impoverished, and the land concentrating in the hands of capitalists . . . The fruits of the toil of millions are boldly stolen to build up colossal fortunes for a few, unprecedented in the history of mankind; and the possessors of those, in turn, despise the Republic and endanger liberty. From the same prolific womb of governmental injustice we breed the two great classes – tramps and millionaires.
>
> . . . A vast conspiracy against mankind has been organized on two continents, and is rapidly taking possession of the world. If not met and overthrown at once it forebodes terrible social convulsions, and destruction of civilization, or the establishment of an absolute despotism.
>
> We have witnessed for more than a quarter of a century the struggles of the two great political parties for power and plunder, while grievous wrongs have been inflicted upon the suffering people. We charge that the controlling influences dominating both these parties have permitted the existing dreadful conditions to develop without serious effort to prevent or restrain them.
>
> Assembled on the anniversary of the birthday of the nation . . . we seek to restore the government of the Republic to the hands of 'the plain people,' with which class it originated. We assert our purposes to be identical with the purposes of the National Constitution; to form a more perfect union and establish justice, insure domestic tranquillity, provide for the common defence, promote general welfare, and secure the blessings of liberty for ourselves and our posterity.
>
> (People's Party 1978: 90–2)

Resonating throughout the preamble are the populist themes of moral decay, of a conniving elite, of the essential goodness of ordinary people, of conspiracy, of betrayal. Both in general tone and content, the preamble is illustrative of the frustrations, anxieties and aspirations of populist thinking. In more specific terms, the preamble draws out the themes of reference back to founding ideas and possibilities of the United States in the face of a slipping back, and of retreat from those lofty ideals. It reveals the very American nature of American populism.

The case of populism in the nineteenth-century USA is often seen as *the* example of populism. The literature on its history is voluminous, and the interpretations are almost as numerous. The history of the People's Party and the populist movement has been portrayed as reactionary and nativist on the one hand (Hofstadter 1955), or, very differently, as the first stirrings of progressive politics in the USA, a movement of great 'democratic promise' (Goodwyn 1976). In whatever way it is viewed, the history of the People's Party represented an extremely unusual period in the history of US politics.

The result of the Civil War (1861–65) was to leave a cross-hatching of regional, cultural and economic conflicts as the abiding basis for American politics. The Populists grew up from, out of and across this particular pattern of politics. It is important to understand the context that gave rise to the populist movements, and that takes us back to the Civil War and its legacy.

The war had seen defeat for the South, and the scar of the North–South divide remained as an abiding reminder of the conflict. The distinction represented in many ways the urban North against the rural South. The war had resulted largely from the South's reliance on slavery to sustain its economy, but the division between North and South fed off a series of divisions that were both beyond and embodied by the conflict over slavery. The distinction was between an urban North containing political and financial centres of power, and the South which relied on cotton as its main product and which remained an agrarian society with distinct values and culture. The populist movement was initially a Southern movement but its fate was tied to how far it could extend its reach to the West.

The second division was money. The Civil War had a profound impact on the politics of money. During the war, Congress had created a national banking system and had introduced the paper currency in the form of the greenback. After the Civil War, the government had to deal with the controversy over money that resulted from making money representative of something rather than itself embodying value, and from the cost of the war on different sections of the US economy. The key question concerned whether currency should be representative of gold reserves or whether it should remain as paper money as it was during the war. Government policy was to seek economic growth to make up the difference between the value of paper money issued in the war and

the value of the gold reserves. This placed the farmers in an appal-
ling situation because they had to produce and sell more to gain the
same income (Goodwyn 1976: 13–14). Southern farmers had been
defeated in war and now faced economic ruin.

The third division was between land and industry. Although this
was partially bound up with the North–South divide, the development of an industrial infrastructure in the shape of telegraph
communications and the railroads, the divisions between urban
industrial labour and agricultural workers and farmers, and the
growing power of financiers and bankers were crucial shaping
factors in the economy, politics and society of the USA in the
second half of the nineteenth century. Populists attempted to make
common cause with labour. Sometimes this yielded alliances such
as in the state of Illinois, but this was exceptional. More often than
not, the coalition was at best unsteady and at worst stillborn.

The final line was drawn in the party system. Political compe-
tition was between the Republicans, the party of Lincoln, the party
of the North, and the Democrats as the more conservative of the
parties, defenders of the South, of slavery, and of states' rights. The
parties were regional forces and still bear the imprimatur of their
origins. The parties also wrestled with different positions on money
(Ritter 1997: 34–47). The Republicans moved squarely to financial
conservatism (keeping standards). The Democrats faced fragmentation largely on regional terms, with the Eastern wing of the party
being, in line with the Eastern banking establishment, for financial
conservatism, while Western and Northwestern elements of the
party became advocates of more radical monetary policies. An
uneasy compromise prevailed around different local positions in
the face of the reality of silver as the compromise between gold and
greenbacks. By the time Grover Cleveland was Democratic president for the second time, the uneasy compromise between different sections of the party fell apart. The year 1893 saw a depression
brought on by banking, investment and agricultural crises. Silver
was blamed, and Cleveland reverted to his roots and determined to
maintain the gold standard. This caused the disputes in the party to
flare up and so, by the time of the 1896 election, Cleveland had been
shunted aside and the party was led by a silverite presidential candidate.

The party system embodied cleavages and lines of conflict born
before and of the Civil War. By the 1890s, on a key issue of politics,
the division was not between the Democrats and Republicans but

between these parties and populist sentiment, the movement and even anti-monopolist factions within the Democratic Party. There was a misfit between the two-party system and the politics of the day.[1] The Populists therefore had the potential to realign the party system around them.

The key strategic dilemma for the Populists was therefore in their attitude towards the Democrats. As the party of the South, they were either a potential partner for Populists or a fundamental threat. As financial conservatives they were enemies, but as silverites they were potential allies. In the end, after establishing themselves as an independent force, the Populists made the fatal choice of partnership, but the history of the People's Party was one of real possibility at its outset.

The rise of the Populist movement and the People's Party represented the mobilization of a particular regionally-based defence of agrarian radicalism against the economic and political power of the North and against the failure of the party system to represent this new force. The People's Party was not the first independent force in the era after the Civil War. Indeed there are strong lines of continuity to some of their independent forebears. The Greenback Party lasted from 1876 until 1884. It was by no means insignificant. It gained 13.8 per cent of the national vote in 1878, marking the party's high-water mark. But its real importance lay its anti-monopolitist legacy that formed a platform for populists. They advocated paper money as a means of keeping up with increasing population and the growing economy. In addition, they identified the banking system as against their interests. The party's radicalism, ideas and constituency served as the basis of subsequent populist mobilization.

The mobilization of the Populist movement in its own right started with the Farmers' Alliance. This national movement had its origins in the Texas Alliance formed in 1877. It was an attempt to give farmers a degree of self-reliance and control over their lives and products by moving them away from the lien system of credit which predominated in Southern states. The lien system was a means by which farmers were able to purchase the means of their living even in hard times. The cost of this was that the farmers were forced to produce cotton by the stores who would give them credit based on the promise of the next year's harvest.

The Alliance constructed a system that moved the farmers towards cooperation with each other and towards self-reliance. A similar system had been built up by the Granger Movement in the 1870s which had instituted a systems of cash-only cooperative stores (Goodwyn 1976: 45). This had failed because the farmers did not always have the cash. The Alliance system therefore attempted to link farmers in a commitment to their own trade store and to collectively selling their cotton. To this end Alliance lecturers travelled across Texas encouraging farmers to establish their own sub-alliances. The Alliance fostered a sense of consciousness among farmers, encouraged the development of a political critique and practically created an environment in which individuals and groups could develop into a nascent populist force.

By 1884 the Alliance in Texas was actively debating whether it should become more political, but in its resolutions it had already crossed the line from being a cooperative movement to being a political movement. Its programme attacked the banking and finance system, the railroads, foreign speculators, and demanded recognition for trade unions and cooperative stores, and put forward Greenback ideas (Goodwyn 1976: 79–81). It sought to build a political alliance with the Knights of Labor as the representative of labour.

The movement spread out of Texas into the rest of the South and West. Farmer-lecturers of the Alliance mounted a campaign of recruitment and education. They advised how to set up local democratic organizations (sub-alliances) and how to establish and link into the Alliance system of centralized buying and selling cooperatively (Goodwyn 1976: 91). By 1887 the Alliance inaugurated itself as a national organization. It began to operate as a collective organization for buying cotton and selling to export buyers, so bypassing the lien system which had reinforced farmers in their dependence on cotton (Hicks 1961: 40–1).

As the movement spread it became clear that, for farmers, the railroads and the Eastern banking establishment were at the heart of a system that seemed to systematically cheat farmers and hold them in thrall to interests other than their own. The railroads, farmers reasoned, should offer an opportunity for farmers to sell their harvests widely, and yet the high cost of the railroads meant that the farmers felt themselves to be no better off. The financial system, by fixing the dollar to gold in the face of increasing population and economic growth, meant that the farmers were having to produce more just to stay in the same situation (Goodwyn 1976: 115). The Alliance movement represented a practical solution to pressing problems for some farmers, but it fostered a consciousness that allowed a collective, and ultimately political, critique of the conditions that had given rise to those very problems in the first place.

In 1889 a major figure in the Alliance, Charles Macune, put forward the sub-treasury plan. This was an ambitious and radical plan designed to allow all farmers to cooperate on a local level, so that they could be provided with credit to secure their needs for the coming year and a guaranteed market for their cotton through the Alliance's exchange system (Goodwyn 1976: 127). In the face of the banks' refusals to lend money to the Alliance on the basis of the sub-treasury plan, Macune was forced to suggest a system of treasury notes which would effectively serve as a system of currency. This reinforced the Greenback ideology within the movement as it proved once again to the farmers that the financial system was pitted against their interests. By 1889 the Texas Exchange, unable to match the cooperative efforts of farmers with the support of the banks, collapsed (Goodwyn 1976: 145–6).

The Texas Alliance, while the most important, was only one of a number. Agrarian radicalism was more widespread than that. In Illinois, the Dakotas, Minnesota and Kansas, farmers created cooperative alliances. By 1890 Kansas had seen the formation of a People's Party in the state which had achieved a measure of electoral success (Nugent 1963: 91). Things were different for the Southern Alliance. Meeting in Ocala, Florida, in 1890 the Southern Alliance deliberated about the possibility of a third-party challenge to the Democrats and Republicans, but the strong links between the Southern members of the Alliance and the Democratic Party ruled this out. By the time the Alliance met in St Louis in 1892 the decision was very different. The People's Party was formed and Ignatius Donnelly's impassioned speech formed the basis for the preamble of the party, which held its first presidential nominating convention on Independence Day 1892 in Omaha and adopted what came to be known as the Omaha Platform.

The Omaha Platform became the touchstone for the populist movement. The preamble led into the three planks of the Platform – money, transportation and land. On money, the Platform demanded a nationally regulated currency, divorced from banking corporations, and a government-regulated postal bank where the earnings of the people could be safely deposited. There was a demand for 'free and unlimited coinage of silver and gold' which signalled their move away from tying currency to reserves. There were also calls for limited taxation and a progressive income tax. On transportation, the Platform called for government ownership and operation of the railroads. Finally, the Platform called for land, as the source of wealth and the heritage of the people, to be free of speculation and of foreign investment and demanded that all land owned by railroads and other corporations 'in excess of their actual needs' should revert to the government and be held for settlers. The three planks were also followed by a number of resolutions which did not have the same status but which offer an insight into the party's ideology. These resolutions included calls for a secret ballot, tax reform, immigration restrictions, initiative and referendum devices, term limits for the presidency and vice-presidency, and direct election of the Senate (People's Party 1978: 90–6).

The importance of Omaha in launching a national third-party challenge was tempered by the nature of the movement that was launching it. The unevenness of the movement meant that the party had to engage in multiple processes of negotiation at state levels, as local leaders attempted to fashion an inclusive constituency that could sustain its national aspirations. The leadership of the party therefore reflected some very different state party characteristics and was not always representative of the Alliance that was its basis (Goodwyn 1976: 312). In coming together for the nomination of a presidential candidate, the party elected a former Union general.

The candidate, General James Weaver, polled over a million votes in the 1892 election, but Grover Cleveland, the Democratic candidate, was elected president. The momentum was there for the new party but the cooperative enterprise, so important to the party, was having more and more difficulties. Its lack of access to credit, and therefore the fate of the People's Party, became so important to the movement because it was the only way to unlock the national institutions and make the sub-treasury plan a reality. A number of People's Party candidates did make it to Congress, but that number was small and did not constitute a breach of the wall around national politics constituted by the Democrats and Republicans.

The party had to face not only the internal problems of organization but also a change in the context of politics as the Democrats moved towards a free silver position. William Jennings Bryan, a silverite, was nominated as the Democratic presidential candidate for the 1896 election. In the meantime a struggle had broken out in the People's Party between those who wanted to build a coalition with silverites in the Democratic and Republican parties and those who did not. For this strategy it was seen as necessary to narrow the party's platform around silver so that it would lose the commitments contained in the Omaha Platform. This faced protracted and vociferous opposition from those keen to retain the agrarian radicalism of the party. Once the Democrats nominated Bryan, the silverites were pushed to move the party to declare Bryan the People's Party nominee. They won at the 1896 St Louis convention and Bryan was nominated. He accepted the nomination of the People's Party after great deliberation on his part.

Bryan took his time to accept the nomination, eventually doing so on the basis of the Democratic platform and with a financier and ex-banker as his vice-presidential running-mate. Bryan was defeated in the presidential election and the People's Party collapsed. In accepting Bryan as the populist candidate, the People's Party had moved away from its core ideological basis embodied in the Omaha Platform. It moved towards the single-issue compromise over money and into an unbalanced union with the Democrats that saved the Democratic Party but killed the People's Party. Bryan's defeat in the election sounded the death-knell for the People's Party and for populism as an independent force in US politics.

The experience of the People's Party illustrates many key populist themes. The failure of the party and the movement by no means spelled the end of populist ideas in US politics. They continued to permeate the language, tone and even subsequent movements and moments in US history. The fate of the party at the end of the nineteenth century does point us to a recurrent characteristic of populist movements. The ambivalence about becoming an institutionalized part of politics, as most clearly represented in the backing of Bryan, the Democrat, caused a fundamental weakness in the way the movement mobilized. Joining forces with a part of the establishment had the benefit of side-stepping many of the problems of organizing a segmented, diffuse and pluralist movement but it came at the cost of independence of this most independent of forces.

The People's Party was constructed across key dividing lines of politics in the aftermath of the Civil War. On the one hand this was a driving force for the movement. The Populist movement and the People's Party's very existence was a testimony to the misalignment of the parties with the concerns of ordinary rural American citizens.

They drew on alienation from the party system and from politics in general. On the other hand, it was difficult terrain on which to situate itself and build a mass movement. The history of the movement and the party was to be one of regional, ideological and sectional conflicts. On the rocks of these internal schisms and the shifting ground of politics the People's Party eventually foundered. Maintaining links with the true heartland of rural America and with the simple common sense of its constituency became much more difficult for the movement as it moved into party politics, into compromise, and eventually into political obscurity.

The Populists in the USA were a true mass movement. Compared with populist moments elsewhere in history, it is clear that the star of populism was not tied to the charismatic personalized leadership of one particular individual. There were leaders aplenty with such appeal, but the history of their influence is separate from that of the wider movement. Richard Hofstadter (in Berlin *et al.* 1968: 143) notes that there was no great theorist for American Populism, and Lawrence Goodwyn (1976: 310) ascribes part of the Populist failure to a lack of a social theory that could have been built on top of the ideas of economic cooperation. The mass nature of the movement compounded the ideological difficulties towards institutionalization. Differences between the regional and state movements determined that, at key events, the Populist history was one of the compromise of politics rather than the embodiment of ideological fervour. At the heart of division lay the commitment of Southern Populists to the party of the South, the Democrats, while the Western populists, led by the Kansas Populists, were more committed to the creation of a real third party force that would lever the farmers away from their historical allegiances.

The Populist challenge sprang from a real sense of economic crisis among farmers. The crisis was that they were unable to sustain themselves from the land. The Alliance was the attempt to construct a way out of the crisis by direct means, but it was an attempt that was frustrated by a number of factors, including the unwillingness of financial institutions to extend credit to the fledgling cooperative enterprise. Feeding into this was the more general financial crisis, and the currency issue, which moulded the bankers, railroad companies and land speculators together into a set of demons for the farmers. The reshaping of politics after the Civil War contributed to the sense of crisis as the party system offered a poor fit with the concerns of Southern and Western agricultural radicals.

In the face of these challenges, the Populists drew back into rural America and ideas of the heartland. Their ideas resonated with images of the farmers as productive and dutiful citizens and as the repository of the original ideas of the American revolution as creating a republic of self-governing farmers. The faith that the US Populists placed in the people was no mere abstraction. Macune's sub-treasury plan laced together farmers in a network of trust and cooperation. The cooperative project was an attempt to embody the virtues of the heartland in a practical political project. This was easier to achieve as a cooperative movement than as a political party.

What made the Populist movement unusual in the larger setting was that, because of its basis in the Alliance, any antipathy towards institutions was highly selective. While the Populists rejected the financial institutions and local economic institutions, they attempted to construct their own complex set of alternative institutions. That set of institutions was not without its problems, but it is unusual for populists to construct complex structures.

The legacy of the People's Party was twofold. Firstly, the almost successful attempt to establish populism as an independent force outside the two-party system was a crucial factor in the subsequent realignment of that two-party system (Burnham 1970). While the parties remained and their labels persisted, the whole agenda of US politics was transformed, culminating in Roosevelt's New Deal with the parties coming to represent some wholly new coalitions of constituencies and ideological positions. The Populists served as markers of coming change.

The second legacy of the People's Party was to establish a tone of politics that fitted neatly into the prevailing political culture. The muted radicalism of populism, the drawing back from revolution in favour of radical reform, works very well within the context of politics in the USA. The importance of 'Americanism' as a cornerstone for nearly all political discourse in the USA allows, even encourages, reformists to use populist patterns of politics.

Huey Long and George Wallace

Louisiana's most famous son, Huey Long, was born in the parish of Winn in 1893. The time and the place were important. Two years before, Winn had sent a representative to the Cincinnati convention that drew together agrarian spokesmen in an attempt to

fashion an alternative politics to that of the two main parties. The
representative from Winn came to Cincinnati with signatures of
support from 1200 constituents in a parish with a total adult population of 1531 (Goodwyn 1976: 334). Populism flourished in Winn
and in Louisiana, and it provided both some of the roots of Long's
own politics and the background within which he was to rise so
effectively. The year was one of economic depression across the
USA and it was when the appeal of the Populist movement was
growing. Long was a Populist but was to fashion his populism
through the Democratic Party.

Eschewing the populism of the agrarian movement, Long
entered politics as a Democrat. From the outset of his political
career, he railed against the concentration of wealth and the resulting inequality of social conditions and particularly of the nature of
education (Long 1933: 37–9). Long ranged himself against Wall
Street and the big corporations such as Standard Oil. He campaigned for roads and schools. This was not an unimportant consideration in a poor, rural state. He called for more schoolbooks for
children and for better institutions for the mentally ill (Hair, 1991:
151). Once he attained office he pushed through legislation that
provided free schoolbooks. He raised bonds to spend money on
roads and bridges (Hair 1991: 162). He introduced night schools to
combat adult illiteracy (Hair 1991: 228). From his position as a
senator, Long launched an ambitious scheme to redistribute wealth
in the USA through the Share Our Wealth Society, which proposed
to cap excessive wealth and ensure a basic level of income at the
other end of the scale.

Long was a man of great presence and energy. This was reflected
in the way he operated in power. He cajoled, bullied, made deals,
issued threats and sometimes used the sheer force of his personality to achieve legislation that met his goal. On race, a key issue for
his state, Long straddled the divide. He tried to keep the support
of the Ku-Klux-Klan supporters who were propounding anti-
Catholicism in addition to their message of racism. At the same
time he worked hard not to alienate the substantial Catholic population that was opposed to the Klan (Hair 1991: 128–35). He signed
bills that enforced the racial segregation of the South (Hair 1991:
165). He was afraid of being seen in league with the black population and was not immune from going to the extreme of attempting to stigmatize political opponents for associating with blacks
(Hair 1991: 223). For all his concern for the poor, he did little for

the black population of his state and even increased the disparity between black and white education levels by the time he left the governorship (Hair 1991: 228). Long was not above altering his message to suit those that came to hear him. Towards the end of his life (he was assassinated in 1935) he had centralized power in Louisiana to such an extent that he had become a dictator. He resented this accusation, arguing that he could not be a dictator if he acted in the interests of the people (Hair 1991: 294).

Throughout his political life Long cultivated a folksy image, entreating voters to call him by his first name (Hair 1991: 201), ignoring the rules of decorum in the Senate (Hair 1991: 234), and backing the widow of a senator and effectively propelling Mrs Caraway to a miraculous victory as the first woman elected to a full Senate term in US history (Hair 1991: 247–8). His dress was as colourful as his language, and it can be little surprise that he pro-voked threats of physical violence from senators as much as from less austere opponents. He made much of his knowledge of the Bible and of his ignorance of the writings of economists (Hair 1991: 271).

The roots of Southern populism emerged again in the 1950s and 1960s. The election of George Wallace as governor of Alabama in 1963 brought into power a populist who had begun his political career, in his own words, 'talking about schools and highways and prisons and taxes' (quoted in Carter 1995: 109). By the time he came to national prominence, he had discovered the resonance and power of the issue of race. In his inaugural speech as governor of Alabama after a campaign that proved the potential of appealing to anti-federal and anti-black sentiments, Wallace famously declared: 'Segregation now . . . segregation tomorrow . . . segrega-tion forever'. He had taken a position which was ideologically in favour of racial segregation and opposed to civil rights; in 1963 he physically took a position in front of the entrance to the University of Alabama in Tuscaloosa as he attempted to prevent blacks regis-tering for the first time. Wallace was forced to back down and the first two black students registered. Wallace was defeated in Tuscaloosa, but defeat at the hands of the Kennedy administration in Washington was grist to his populist mill.

Wallace's style, as befitting an ex-boxer, was pugnacious and bombastic. He cultivated an image of ordinariness. He dressed in cheap suits, slicked his hair back and professed his predilection for country music and 'ketchup on everything' (Kazin 1995: 235). He

had worked his way up to national prominence through election as
a state legislator in 1947 before becoming governor. He worked his
way through the party of the South, the Democrats, but it had
become the vehicle of the Eastern liberal establishment and
Wallace, after contesting a number of presidential primaries in
1964, formed his own party and ran for the presidency in 1968 as
an independent candidate. The party was nothing more than a
vehicle for Wallace but, standing on a platform of increased social
security, improved health services, union rights and implied racism
of a backlash against the federal agenda of civil rights (Lipset and
Raab 1971: 346–8), he succeeded in garnering 13.5 per cent of the
vote and winning in five Southern states.

Wallace's politics in the 1960s mixed three things. Most famously,
there was his support for segregation and therefore a clear politics
of race. The second element was his distrust of the establishment.
His hostility extended from the new liberal political establishment
to banks and the rich. He regularly spluttered against 'bureaucrats',
'theoreticians' and 'pseudo-intellectuals'. The final element was a
defence of those he saw as outside the establishment. This defence
meant opposition to the federal government's imposition on the
states of policies that they did not agree with. But it also meant that
Wallace advocated tax reform designed to benefit his natural constituency of the white Southern farmers (Lesher 1994: 476).

To understand the politics of Wallace it is vital to understand the
context of US politics during the 1960s. Much of Wallace's zeal was
focused on the defence of his natural constituency in the face of
change. His agenda of states' rights reflected his affinity for the
already existing heartland of Alabama (or rather, a certain white
vision of rural Alabama). Change threatened the heartland. That
change came from the federal government but also from the social
movements of civil rights and of the new left in general. Wallace's
defensive reactionary populism owed as much to the challenge of
new social movements as it did to what was being defended.
Wallace was rallying to defend his heartland in the face of the challenge of the new left.

After his bid for the presidency in 1968 Wallace turned his attention back to gaining the governorship of Alabama, and did so in
1970. Once in office he began to move away from the politics of race
(Lesher 1994: 457) and back into the fold of the Democratic Party,
and contested a number of presidential primaries in 1972. In Maryland he was shot. This put him in a wheelchair and out of the

election. Although he won the Maryland primary the day after the shooting, he did not win the Democratic nomination. He continued as governor of Alabama, winning the support of blacks in the state, and contested the 1976 presidential election. He publicly apologized in 1982 for his previous behaviour towards black citizens (Lesher 1994: 501).

The movement of Wallace's position demonstrates the relationship between the politics of race and populism in the USA. Just as the experience of the People's Party in the 1890s has given rise to very different interpretations of the movement's relationship to the race question (Hofstadter 1955; Goodwyn 1976), so Wallace's shift raises ambiguities. What it demonstrates is that populism, because it is heavily dependent on the context which gives rise to it, will change with that context. It also demonstrates that there is nothing essentially racist in populism, although populists may be racist and will often practice the politics of exclusion through creating a constituency that is defined in terms of who is excluded rather than who is included. Wallace was defending his vision of the heartland that was embodied in a version of white rural God-fearing Alabama. The exclusion of blacks from that vision was due to the history of the Southern states and Wallace's populism, through constructing a heartland through reference to the past, inevitably embodied the racial divide.

The change in the context of US politics between 1968 and 1982 was twofold. Firstly, the agenda of civil rights became both institutionally embodied in the acts of all three branches of government and became socially far less divisive. The other change was that Nixon, Carter and Reagan all realized the potential of a tempered populism as a strategy for attaining presidential office. Nixon's hostility towards the media and the Eastern establishment was echoed in Jimmy Carter's campaign which focused on his own status as an outsider. Reagan's emphasized anti-intellectualism and good old common sense. Wallace had had his populist thunder stolen as it became a recurrent part of US presidential politics.

Populism in contemporary US politics

In the campaign for the 1992 presidential election, Ross Perot emerged as an independent candidate. As a Texan billionaire businessman, Perot hardly appeared the populist archetype of anti-elitist, but in the way he campaigned and in what he campaigned for, Perot's presence revealed the persistence of populism in US politics. He gained one-fifth of the vote in what was the most successful third-party campaign for 80 years.

Perot's frustration with politicians and parties showed through in his bombastic style. Mixing a suffused sense of anger with simple homilies and homespun language, Perot built his appeal around offering common sense and a business mind to the 'business' of politics. Perot stressed the national debt and the need to have a plan to redress it. The use and importance of this issue is illustrative of how Perot was effectively invoking the common sense of the household or of the business environment to address an issue that he felt the politicians were deliberately ignoring. He called for the USA to lessen its international commitment and he trumpeted the importance of term limits for politicians. The issues and the style drew in those voters who were disenchanted with the other parties and who had a distrust in politics, but it was the presence of Perot that was important to those that were initially mobilized behind his campaign (Gold 1995: 763–4; McCann *et al.* 1999: 25).

Perot claimed that he did not want to run but felt obligated to. His initial candidacy only happened following a television interview and after he had secured the support of the members of his organization in a poll. This political reluctance was to emerge again in the 1992 campaign. He withdrew suddenly in the summer but quickly re-entered the race. This reinforced his image of reluctance and therefore was a populist gesture designed to stress how far Perot was not naturally of the world he was seeking to enter, the political world, but was being forced into it by the failure of its current occupiers.

Around him Perot initially built the United We Stand America organization as the embodiment of his message. In classic populist style, he achieved this through reaching out to non-aligned voters and to those who traditionally had felt themselves excluded. The 'We' in 'United We Stand America' is, again in classic populist style, left implicit and reveals a rallying cry to the heartland. The use of Perot's own substantial wealth made possible a large campaign of recruitment that yielded a genuinely popular response.[2] He set up a toll-free telephone number to recruit activists and used paid 'infomercials' to put across his message. He spent over $60 million from his own pocket on the campaign, refusing federal subsidies.

Perot's input into the 1992 presidential election was to pay off: he achieved almost 19 per cent of the vote, with 20 million electors choosing him. This was the best third-party showing since Theodore Roosevelt's Progressive campaign in 1912. Subsequently United We Stand America became transformed into the Reform Party, and the party has become a minor force in US politics.

Perot and his movement are simply the latest in a long line of populist movements in the USA. His prominence in politics, however fleeting, may owe as much to a populist heritage and to a certain fit between populist ideas and US political culture as it does to his personality. This should not blind us to the source of his appeal. Contemporary populist politics in the US is indicative of some sort of problem with the functioning of the political system. The nature of that problem and the possible solutions may vary widely, but populism should still be treated as a gauge of the health of representative politics.

The United States gives us the best example of a populist movement in the true sense of being a bottom-up phenomenon built through a genuinely mass movement. Burgeoning into the most significant third-party challenge to the dominance of the Democrats and Republicans, the People's Party represented the politics of mass populism in practice. The party had risen on the most American of themes and yet remained essentially populist. This is no contradiction as there has been a continual theme of populism running through American politics (Kazin 1995). After the demise of the People's Party in 1896, populism in the US found no immediate political expression but was to re-emerge with regularity in different political episodes in the twentieth century.

The populist moments in US political history have been founded on frustration with economic or political institutions. Populist movements have usually (but not exclusively) been movements outside the parameters of the party system: independent forces of protest. The frustration with political institutions has made populists attempt to innovate in the forms that they use. At one extreme, the People's Party was founded on grass-roots democratic politics built out of a radical cooperative movement. At the other extreme, in Long and Wallace, populism resolved its antipathy towards institutions by effectively replacing them with movements based almost exclusively on the appeal of personalized leadership.

In the People's Party's initial reluctance to enter into politics and in its final act in 1896 of effectively joining with the Democrats, the movement revealed its fundamental ambivalence about being an

independent political party rather than a spontaneous social movement of protest and cooperation. The waning of Wallace's political
star and the electoral difficulties of Perot's Reform Party similarly
indicate the limits of being an independent political force even
when heavily dependent on highly personalized leadership.

The importance to US populism of a sense of crisis has not
changed. The particular crisis may well have changed, but the populist response has been remarkably consistent. The economic crisis
in agriculture that hit Southern and Western farmers in the era after
the Civil War provided the momentum for the populist movement
of that era. In the twentieth century the antagonism of the USA to
world-wide communism reached its apogee in the Cold War. When
the divisions engendered by this on the international scene combined with the social and civil unrest over race and civil rights on
the domestic scene, it provided a tinderbox atmosphere for the
populism of George Wallace, and he exploited the divisions created
by this sense of crisis to the full. Perot's populism draws deeply
from the well of economic anxiety that has been engendered in the
US by globalization. His isolationism and protectionism derive
from his attempt to shore up US economic security in a world
economy that has been seen to only provide economic insecurity.

In the USA, the concept of the heartland finds its clearest explicit
presence in populist rhetoric and thought. The idea of a productive
and dutiful rural heartland was a powerful idea for the populists in
the nineteenth century. One of the most powerful effects of the
Populist movement in the nineteenth century was to give expression and legitimacy to the claims of the rural South after the defeat
in the Civil War. It is no coincidence that both Long and Wallace
drew their political bases from the South and were definitively
Southern politicians. The heartland of the USA has consistently
been the simple virtues of the rural states as against the industrial
cosmopolitanism of the Eastern seaboard. Only once the New Deal
electoral coalitions that underlay the two main parties came apart
was there an opportunity for a more geographically inclusive conception of the heartland, as evoked by Perot in his campaign against
the political establishment embodied in Washington, DC.

It is fitting that the USA holds so much material for the study of
populism. The US political system was originally established on the
basis of building a polity around the ideas of representative politics. The debates of the 'founding fathers' and the ideas developed
have themselves become an integral part of debate about the

meaning of modern democratic politics. The ideas of populism and its instinctive reaction against the institutions of representative politics have found fertile ground in US politics.

The very American nature of populism, the constant reference to the founding ideas of the nation and the recurrent plaintive tone of romantic reference to the loss of innocence and of direction, reveals the chameleonic nature of populism. That American populism is seen as more American than populist is testimony to the powers of absorption in populism. At different periods of US politics, populism has taken on different issues at its core, but what has remained consistent is the way in which those issues have been framed and the resonance of these with significant sections of the American public.

Notes

1 The disenfranchisement of Southern blacks meant that another fault-line of American politics, that of race, was to remain dormant until black populations became formally and effectively enfranchised.
2 There are strong echoes of the way in which another rich businessman, Silvio Berlusconi constructed his populist political organization, Forza Italia, in Italy.

4

To the People!
Lessons from
Russian Populism

In the summer of 1874 in Russia there was a spontaneous movement of young men and women from the cities to the countryside.
They came from the universities and they went with zeal and con-
viction into rural Russia. Fired up by the writings and admonishments of intellectuals and theorists and convinced of the need to
bring about fundamental change in their country, to transform the
old order with a revolutionary vision, they went to proselytize, to
teach, but mainly to catalyse the peasantry into rebellion against
the tsarist regime. Above all, the young intellectuals were propelled
by a belief that it was in the peasantry that lay the great wisdom of
the Russian past and so also hope for the future.

The students were following Alexander Herzen's exhortation,
made a decade earlier, to go to the people. Their project ended in
failure. Eventually the students were to lose faith in the immediate
revolutionary potential of the peasantry and they turned to terrorism in an attempt to bring down the state, but while holding fast to
the idea that Russia's future lay with the peasantry. This movement
and its ideas were interpreted as precursors of the revolutionary
movement which culminated in the Bolshevik uprising of 1917.
Certainly the ideas of the *narodniki*, as they were known, were a
crucial ingredient in the peculiar mix of revolutionary thought that
attracted the Russian intelligentsia in the period. For our purposes,
Russian populism has a different importance. It is the clearest
example of the romanticization of the rural lifestyle and of the
attempt to build a movement on that basis. What makes this so
clear is that the peasantry were revered from outside – by a part of

the elite. The *narodniki*, for their part, were drawn from the urban elite of tsarist Russia and sought a social ideal well outside their own world.

Russian populism: *narodnichestvo* and the *narodniki*

The peasant class had found itself both heavily exploited and the principal object of political discussion in Russia. Tsar Alexander II, while no liberal, had seen the need to change the situation of the serfdom of the peasantry. 'It is better to abolish serfdom from above than to wait until the serfs begin to liberate themselves from below', he had declared in 1856 (Seton-Watson 1967: 335). To pre-empt such a movement, he emancipated the serfs in 1861, giving them freedom from the landowners and the right to own land. The Emancipation had the effect of not really improving the peasants' lot as they had to buy the rights to their land and were hardly in a position to do so, and these 'Redemption Payments' became a huge burden on the peasantry at a time when it was already becoming increasingly difficult to sustain a living through agriculture (Pipes 1995: 165–8). The Emancipation Proclamation did reflect the widespread concern that this great mass of Russian people held the future of the country in their hands, but it was short of delivering land, freedom and the future directly into their grasp.

While the Emancipation of the serfs did not free the peasantry in the way the *narodniki* wanted, it did have the effect of reinforcing peasant structures that were to serve as a fundamental source of inspiration for the *narodniki*. The running of tsarist Russia relied on the feudal system, which depended on the administrative role of the landowners. Taking their position away in the Emancipation meant that a new administrative machinery had to come about to replace them. At the level of the peasantry this structure came in the form of the village communes (*obshchina*). Peasant village communes were already embedded in Russian rural culture and traditions. In a narrow sense, *obshchina* referred to a grouping of peasants who held land and who co-operated as part of a *mir* which was an assembly of peasant householders meeting to make decisions. In the more general sense, *obshchina* was an idealized egalitarian peasant community (Grant 1976: 636–7).

The idea of the *obshchina* played a central role in Russian populist thought. It anchored a revolutionary ethos that was internationally widespread to an institution that was fundamentally

Russian. The crucial aspects of the *obshchina* for the populists were that they were self-governing, based on collective landownership by the peasantry and bound together with a sense of community that stressed egalitarianism. This most Russian of structures embodied not only a way of organizing but, just as importantly, an ethos, and the possibility of seeing the peasantry as a potential force for freedom rather than as a backward-looking and reactionary force.

The very term 'populism' has a disputed and disputatious lineage in the Russian case. Drawing on the term *narod*, meaning something like the German concept of *Volk*, the term came in the 1860s and 1870s to denote a movement, stressing both its popular and its democratic roots (Pipes 1964: 443). It was only after the 'Going to the People' movement that the terms for the ideology (*narodnichestvo*) and for its adherents (*narodniki*) came into wide usage. Even then the terms were used to cover some different sets of ideas. Richard Pipes (1964) sums up the variation by suggesting that it was used in two distinct senses. First, it was used to describe the notion that the masses were superior to the educated elite, leading to a 'grass-roots, pragmatic theory of collective action' (Pipes 1964: 458). A second sense is where it was used to describe those who believed that Russia had its own indigenous possibility of reaching socialism through bypassing capitalism. The latter sense was largely confined to Marxist debate, but the first has the most resonance with populism as used in other settings. In practice it is difficult always to sustain a hard and fast distinction between the two meanings.[1]

Alexander Herzen and the foundations of Russian populism

The central ideas of Russian populism were generated in the debates of the Russian intelligentsia. Nourished by the desire for revolutionary change pervasive among many intellectuals of the time both in Russia and in Europe, and a belief in the exceptional nature of Russian society, Russian revolutionary thought charted a tortuous course through some very different individual thinkers and strategies until the Leninist version of Marxism prevailed in the 1917 Revolution. The belief in the exceptional nature of Russian social institutions, and specifically of the virtues of the forms of social and economic organization of the Russian peasantry, was neither new nor confined to revolutionary thought. The Slavophile movement of the 1840s and 1850s was a backward-looking conservative romantic movement that stressed the village commune, the need to nurture the sense of the people in Russia and the need for spiritual and religious regeneration (Venturi 1960: 13–19).

Drawing on some of the ideas of the Slavophiles and combining with them a more Western orientation, Alexander Herzen had a major influence of the development of revolutionary thought in the mid-nineteenth century. He left Russia, disillusioned with the lack of revolution in 1848, settling in London in 1852. His influence on revolutionary thought, however, remained in Russia. From England he disseminated his ideas through the establishment of the Free Russian Press and through publishing a journal, *Kolokol* ('The Bell'). The journal was read by revolutionaries and conservatives alike in Russia. In it and through it, Herzen moved Russian revolutionary thought into contact with the Western socialism of Saint-Simon and Fourier, and remained a pivotal figure and touchstone for the Russian revolutionary intelligentsia through the second half of the nineteenth century. It was in its pages, in November 1861, that Herzen laid down the challenge to the intelligentsia which was to be taken up over a decade later: '*to the people, to the people* – there is your place, you exiles from seats of learning. Show that you will become fighters on behalf of the Russian people' (quoted in Ulam 1981: 102).

Herzen's impact went beyond rhetoric. Herzen laid the foundations for Russian populism through some basic principles (Venturi 1960: 35; Berlin 1978: 197–208). The themes were focused around his distrust of liberal democracy, his suspicion of abstractions, his faith in the Russian peasant, and his belief in the need for a dedicated group of revolutionaries. In exploring these themes we can see how they came to propel the activists and the movements associated with Russian populism. It also becomes apparent, when we set the principles alongside the experience of the revolutionary activists, that Herzen's influence did not necessarily always lead towards the sort of strategies, activities and ideas with which populism is usually associated.

Herzen saw government as 'not an end, but a necessity' (quoted in Venturi 1960: 32) and this led to a distrust of the ideals of democracy that he found advocated around him. His time in Europe only hardened his rejection of the Western version of democracy as exemplified in the belief in parliaments and centralized authority only tenuously linked to the people. He saw the need for a revolutionary liberation of the people, but he did not accept that the way to realize this vision was through the structures of liberal representative democracy.

For Herzen, political action was far more important than political institutions. A theme running throughout his life was that political life should not serve abstractions. Ideological abstractions were, for Herzen, fundamentally destructive (Berlin 1978: 193). Populism in many different forms has expressed a hostility towards theory, towards ideology and towards intellectualism. It is obviously difficult for a man whose life was devoted to the propagation of ideas to be fundamentally opposed to that activity, but in Herzen's antipathy towards abstraction he came as close as someone in his position could. Here emerges a common populist dilemma that comes about though theorizing about non-theorizing, which is another version of the difficulty encountered by populists when they become politicians on the basis of their distrust of politicians.

A principle of Herzen that owed more to his particular context was his belief in the possibility of a Russian route to socialism through the peasantry and particularly through his faith in the *obshchina* as the basis for future social organization, and in the possibility of skipping the capitalist phase of development. He saw in the traditional Russian peasant commune the opposite of the acquisitive materialistic bourgeoisie and proletariat that he encountered in Europe (Ulam 1998: 36). Part of the appeal of the Russian peasantry was in the practical usefulness of their organization in the *obshchina*, but part of his faith in the peasantry lay in his belief that they remained uncorrupted by modern capitalist and Western development, unlike the urban working class and the bourgeoisie. The purity of the peasantry was a reflection of their 'innocence' and their untaintedness. Populism often raises the theme of simple people being corrupted by outside and sinister forces. The Russian peasantry and the romanticization of their values by the *narodniki* were therefore easily viewed in this way.

Herzen embodied his belief in political action in the need to foster revolutionary activists who would be dedicated to the people. It was this theme that was taken up by students who went to the people, but, more than this, it was this idea which suffused the revolutionary intellectual class in tsarist Russia, giving them both a purpose and a justification of their role in stirring up the peasantry.

'Going to the People'

The two or three thousand young members of the intelligentsia who went into the countryside in 1874 were intellectually following Herzen's admonishments about being with the people.[2] They were in practice following the example of the Chaikovskists and of Dolgushin and his followers. The Chaikovskists were a small but active group of propagandists who had, since 1870, attempted by means of propaganda to spur on the workers of St Petersburg to rebellion; even more, they were following Alexander Dolgushin, who in 1873 had attempted to revolutionize the peasantry outside Moscow. Dolgushin and a few followers had, putting their faith in propaganda, set up a printing press in a village just outside Moscow. They printed books and pamphlets, distributing them to the peasantry. They attempted to assimilate themselves into rural society through working with the peasantry and then had tried to stir up the peasants' feelings of resentment about their conditions. They found the peasants unresponsive and sometimes hostile. Dolgushin's group were soon discovered by the authorities, arrested and sentenced to ten years' hard labour (Venturi 1960: 496–501; Ulam 1998: 210–14).

The *narodniki* who went to the people in 1874 lacked a written programme or organization. They came from intellectual urban circles and were relatively inexperienced in the business of political work. Moving from village to village, they distributed revolutionary pamphlets and talked indiscriminately to the peasants who crossed their path about the need radically to redistribute land and engage in revolution. In 'Going to the People' they were following the suggestions of revolutionary activists and thinkers, such as Mikhail Bakunin and Peter Lavrov, who sought the way to revolution through the most oppressed and the most numerous. The followers of Bakunin saw the peasantry as a mass to be politicized and taught about how they were being oppressed. The followers of Lavrov saw the task as to become at one with the people, to live with the people and to develop collectively a revolutionary consciousness with the peasantry. In a land such as Russia where the peasantry were 48 million of the total 60 million inhabitants (Pipes 1995: 144) and yet so poor, these seemed like revolutionary strategies.

There was a degree of spontaneity about the 'Going to the People' movement. There was also an atmosphere of piousness that seemed quasi-religious. Ulam (1998) goes so far as to refer to the movement as a pilgrimage. Dolgushin had seen the need to use religious rhetoric in the propaganda, as this was a way of breaking down the social barriers between the intellectuals and the peasants. He used Gospel references in his propaganda. This tone permeated the students as they went into the countryside. It is easy to understand how contemporaries and activists themselves drew comparisons with early Christians, with a small apostolate group moving among and teaching the ordinary people. Faith drove the early Christians, but it was deep faith in the peasantry that drove the *narodniki*.

The euphoria of the *narodniki* came up against two problems. The first and most disheartening for them was the lack of appetite for revolution among the peasantry. The *narodniki* had imagined the peasants to be oppressed, idealistic and ripe for revolution. In practice they found the peasants to be acquisitive, conservative and profoundly suspicious of the students. While the *narodniki* held fast to the idea of the oppression by the tsarist regime, in their contact with the peasantry they found a deeply embedded loyalty towards the tsar.[3] The distance between the students and the peasantry did not help their persuasive powers. Unused to manual work and often without practical skills, the *narodniki* found that living as the peasantry was not an easy proposition and their credibility among the peasantry was not easy to gain.

The second problem for the *narodniki* was that the regime that they had sought to undermine acted against them and arrested 1611 of them between 1873 and 1877, culminating in two trials in 1877 and 1878 (Seton-Watson 1967: 422). The response of the state was made more stinging by the fact that sometimes it was the peasants themselves who turned in the idealistic activists to the authorities. The summer of 1874 showed what a group of activists could do. More than that, it showed what the peasantry would not do.

From the people to the terror

The populists moved their attention away from the peasantry and turned violently towards the state. If the peasantry could not be galvanized into revolution then it was necessary to attack the state as the instrument of the peasantry's repression. The populists were seeking to temper their disappointment in the peasantry with new strategies that might still lead to revolution (Wortman 1967: 189). The shift was away from propaganda and towards terror. Although the activists remained theoretically committed to educating and working among the peasantry, they were, in practice, far more motivated to carry out spectacular acts of violence.

The use of terror relied on a greater degree of organization, and this was provided largely by Mark Natanson. Between 1876 and 1878 he developed a group which became the second incarnation of a group calling itself 'Land and Freedom' (*Zemlya i Volya*) and which became the vehicle for violence against the state.[4] In contrast to the 'Going to the People' movement, Land and Freedom was both centralized and highly organized. The organization was committed to giving land to the people, to smashing the state, to breaking up the Russian empire and to the preservation of the *obshchina* as the basis for a new social order (Venturi 1960: 573–4). Even at the same time as the populists assassinated and planted bombs, they still attempted to theorize their action. Violence was an attempt to be concrete and to move away from the abstraction and intellectualism of the earlier phase of their movement, while at the same time being in tune with the nature of the peasantry (Walicki 1969: 96).

The 'Trial of the 193' accused of revolutionary propaganda during the 'Going to the People' movement ended in 1878 with only 40 being found guilty and was quickly followed by an assassination attempt, albeit unsuccessful, on the unpopular governor of St Petersburg by Vera Zasulich, one of the women who had been part of the 'Going to the People' movement. The subsequent trial turned into an assessment of the governor and Zasulich was found not guilty by her jury, despite having shot the governor at point-blank range. These events had the effect of legitimizing the tactic of more terrorist acts by appearing to offer the endorsement of society through the courts for those engaged in extreme actions (Ulam 1998: 265, 274).

Land and Freedom continued to contribute to the campaign of terror that was marked by assassinations of political figures. Within the movement tensions arose. On the one side were those who wanted to stay true to the *narodnik* vision and to move away from terror for its own sake, and on the other hand there were those who wanted to continue with the terror and to move towards the ultimate act of terror in the assassination of the tsar. Land and Freedom therefore fractured in 1879, with a new grouping, 'People's Will' (*Narodnaya Volya*), emerging to take up the campaign of terror. It did so as part of a wider political engagement which was designed to give it access to power. It published a death sentence on the tsar and began a bombing campaign with this as the goal. After a number of attempts, the group succeeded in 1881. This marked the death of the movement as, under the new Tsar Alexander III, the leaders were arrested, convicted and executed.

By the time People's Will had killed the tsar, the link to populism was only fragmentary. In many ways those from Land and Freedom who rejected the move to terrorism combined with a more 'political' strategy, were closer to *narodnichestvo* because they were closer to Herzen's legacy in privileging the action of propagandizing among the peasantry and rejecting the engagement with political institutions. They united under the name of 'Black Repartition' (*Chernyi Peredel*), but they were seen as moving back to the failures of the early 1870s and they did not represent a revolutionary force (Walicki 1980: 233). Certainly the activists of People's Will still claimed to be acting for the people and with the goal of building a system of Russian socialism around peasant communes, but in the strategy they followed, the ideas that drove them, and in their only nominal links to the people, this small group of dedicated terrorists operating under a highly centralized organization had largely left behind the ideas of Russian populism. The ideas and experiences of the *narodniki* had shaped them but they no longer fashioned populist ideas in their struggle.

It is tempting to drop the Russian case from the consideration of populism. It sits uneasily with populism elsewhere, being a movement of elites. A further justification for its exclusion is offered by those scholars who claim that the translation of the word *narodniki* as 'populist' is simply incorrect and that therefore the comparison with North American agrarian radicalism is forced and artificial (Allcock 1971: 372). But to follow this course would be unwise. Whatever issue of translation there is, it is still clear in the Russian case that populist themes emerged powerfully in an unusual context. In the *narodniki*, because of the exceptional circumstances and subsequent history, it is possible more easily to isolate factors which come bound up with other contexts in populism elsewhere. This means that Russian populism is, if viewed carefully, a powerful illuminator of universal elements of populism.

Even if we accept that the *narodniki* should be classed as populist, this does not free us from all the difficult problems of interpretation about the Russian case. The line of differentiation around what constitutes either the *narodniki* or populism is by no means clear-cut. I have not focused mostly on the 'Going to the People' movement because I take it to be the sum total of Russian populism. Indeed if it were the sum total, it would constitute a rather meagre amount: the movement was small, short-lived and profoundly unsuccessful. The 'Going to the People' movement does constitute a high-water mark in Russian populism, or, as Venturi (1960: 470) calls it, the 'real "springtime" of the movement'. We see in it, in the themes from Herzen that it embodied and in the subsequent reversion to terrorism, the continuation of the 'same' struggle by other means and it is only fully comprehensible in the light of the events of 1874, just as the revolutionary fervour of the intelligentsia is only fully comprehensible in the light of their subsequent move to terror.

A major part of the explanation for the difficulty in isolating exactly what constitutes Russian populism lies in the overarching commitment to socialist revolution on the part of the radical intelligentsia of the time. And of course, our perception of tsarist Russia is inevitably tempered by the knowledge that the regime was to be overcome in the Bolshevik uprising in 1917. Taken together, this means that it was at least tempting to see Russian thought in this period solely as a precursor to Marxism-Leninism. This is to oversimplify and to lose, in the process, both the essence of Russian populism and a key feature of Russian revolutionary socialism. The revolutionary socialist thought that eventually won out can only be fully understood in the light of the very Russian nature of revolutionary thought. The emphasis, on the part of the *narodniki*, on the possibility of a unique Russian path to socialism and on the communal values and structure of the *obshchina* resonates through Russian Marxism-Leninism. In the same way, Russian populism must be understood as part of the complex weave of revolutionary socialist ideas. The chameleonic nature of populism in general is exemplified in the case of Russian populism's inextricable linkage with Russian revolutionary socialism.

The wider world of political ideas is by no means irrelevant to understanding the *narodniki*. The context of European political thought is one in which democracy was the driving force behind the thrust of intellectuals and of revolutionaries elsewhere. Sharing the concern of other democrats with overthrowing absolutism, the *narodniki* were nonetheless hostile to the liberal alternative of representative or liberal democracy. As I have suggested above,

Herzen's hostility to this form of democracy was taken up by and, if anything, heightened by the *narodniki*. Understood as a purely Russian phenomenon, it would make little sense to see them as reacting against representative politics as they were reacting not against representation but against the legacy of tsarist absolutist rule. If we draw into the picture the ideas generated outside Russia, it makes more sense to see part of their populism as an attempt to construct a politics that avoided the ethos and structure of liberal representative politics. Indeed it would be strange to try and explain the subsequent fate of Russia without reference to the way in which ideas from Western Europe, including Marxism, were transmuted into Russian forms, so we must do the same for the populists in looking more widely.[5]

In rejecting the ideas of liberal reformist democratic ideas, the *narodniki* were also embodying a deeper antipathy towards politics that was apparent in the thinking of Herzen. Whereas the reluctance of populists to engage in politics often means that they engage in a short-lived and reformist manner in conventional politics, the anti-politics of the *narodniki* meant for them a construction of a wholly new form of action that involved living, teaching and agitating rather than participating in political actions which were based on the assertion of constitutional rights. In the move to terror, the Russian revolutionaries were taking populism to an extreme that it has not otherwise gone to in its attempt to embody antipathy towards politics in anti-political actions.

For the Russian populists, the Russian countryside and the peasantry were their heartland. The idealized conception of Russian rural life, of the ways of the peasantry and of their ways of living and organizing themselves forms a clearly defined and detailed conception of what constitutes the heartland. In the celebration of the *obshchina* the heartland is portrayed as both a way of life, an organizational structure and even a spirit of community.

It is precisely because the *narodniki* were not themselves of the people that we can more clearly see the object of their ideological affections. In other cases, populist movements are drawn from the people they seek to represent. Where the people need to be effectively mobilized from outside it is easier to discern the boundaries of the heartland. As the Russian *narodniki* were drawn from and driven by an intelligentsia and because this meant that they were, by definition, apart from the heartland, it is possible to see the heartland as an explicit conception. In other populist movements or ideas, the heartland remains implicit. Looking at the Russian *narodniki* allows us to see the clearest version of the heartland.

The emphasis on finding a Russian path towards socialism can be seen in both positive and negative lights. Both are clearly populist. The idea of a particularly Russian route to socialism via the inherent wisdom and potential of the peasantry demonstrates the faith in the occupants of this particular heartland. It is also a manifestation of the rejection of external influences. Herzen's antipathy towards Western parliamentarism and towards Western revolutionary theory as exemplified by Marx is illustrative of the hostility that populists feel towards those outside the borders of the heartland. The rejection of liberalism and Marxism can be seen as a rejection of where these ideas were from as well as a rejection of the ideas themselves.

The incident of 'Going to the People' was both short-lived and unsuccessful. The failure of the movement was not due to the difficulties of structuring a populist movement of the people, as they never reached that far. The idea failed to become a popular movement, remaining more as the ideology of a relatively small number of adherents. Its failure to become a mass movement of the people that it revered stems largely from its failure to embrace the reality of those people. Russian populism was chameleonic enough to seek contact with the peasantry, but it stopped short of actually taking up the peasantry's outlook as this would have meant forfeiting the *narodniki*'s commitment to revolution. In the choice between the extremism of populist surrender to the will of the people and the extremism of violent revolution, the *narodniki* chose revolution over populism.

Populism is rarely revolutionary in the true sense of the word. It tends to advocate reform but rarely brings itself to advocate a wholesale replacement of the regime. The Russian *narodniki* were clearly revolutionary in the sense that they wanted to bring about profound social and political change in Russia. They were also revolutionary in the sense that they were part of the context that led to the Bolshevik revolution. On the one hand, we can content ourselves with the comment that the Russian populists were unusually revolutionary in their populism. On the other hand, it is clear that what binds the populists together, and makes them distinct from the other revolutionary currents of the time, is their belief that in the experience and structure of the Russian peasantry there lay true revolutionary potential. The peasant was, for the populists, not only an object to be mobilized for the sake of the revolution but also much more. The populist version of revolution was one that would create change, but that change was *partially* backward-looking. The purpose of populist revolution was to create a regime that would allow a social order that fully realized the potential of the peasantry, and that potential was already partially apparent in Russian history.

The case of Russian *narodnichestvo* sits uneasily with other cases of populism. The muted radicalism of most other populisms is taken to a revolutionary extreme by the *narodniki*'s commitment to socialist revolution. The reverence for the simple peasant life is so clear to see because that reverence did not spring from the peasantry themselves and so cannot be confused with self-interest. The intellectualism of the *narodniki* allows us to glimpse what the potentially oxymoronic notion of theorized populism looks like. But all the theory did not allow them to overcome the practical difficulty of mobilizing the peasantry, and they were overshadowed by the ability of Marxism-Leninism to do just that to great effect.

Notes

1 The literature on Russian populism is, quite correctly, very concerned about the categorization of ideas and individuals. For our purposes, it is less important which ideas or individuals fall precisely into the category of Russian populism but it is more useful to see how Russian populism, as a diverse and changing set of ideas and people, fits with populism more generally.
2 Herzen was not to see his legacy bear fruit, as he died in 1870.
3 The question of the tsar's status was not only an issue for the peasantry. Even revolutionary theorists at times appeared to hold on to the hope that revolution could take place without losing the tsar (Ulam 1998: 44, 64).
4 The first Land and Freedom movement was a small secret conspiratorial movement of about 1000 members committed to giving the peasantry their land and liberty which collapsed in 1863.
5 Walicki (1969; 1980) makes the case that populism in Russia cannot be understood without reference to the influence of Marxism. This claim centres around the contention that Marx's critique of capitalism gave added vigour to the populists' search for a Russian path to socialism that would bypass the evils of capitalism. This assumes that Russian populism is defined, in Pipes' (1964) sense, in terms of its political economy rather than in its broader sense.

5

The Populist Politics of Leadership in Latin America

Populist politics in Latin American illustrates the importance of leadership and, perhaps more than populism elsewhere, is a persistent feature of politics in the region. Populism is present in two senses. First, it is present as a description of sets of regimes and of a type of politics that is part of the Latin American experience. Second, it is used to describe the ideas and history of key leaders who were central to those regimes. In the first sense, Latin American populism has given rise to a number of contextual definitions of populism (see Chapter 2) where populism becomes a common element in the conceptual currency of those analysing Latin American politics. In the second sense, populism is personalized around individuals, the most significant of whom is Juan Perón in Argentina.

Looking at populism in Latin America and regarding Perón as typical, we are offered a rare opportunity to see what happens to populism as a regime. This is important because this is relatively rare in the 'canon' of populist movements, and because populism has real difficulties in regularizing itself as political practices, institutions and regimes. The chameleonic nature of populism means that there are some features that are clearly a product of the context, of the period and of the place. The difficult history of democratic politics in Latin America in the twentieth century means that perhaps a greater emphasis on leadership is to be expected as an antidote to instability. The particular economic and social circumstances of Argentina may go a long way to explaining the policies of redistribution and the ideas of social justice. We need to bear in mind these contextual factors, but this should not crowd out the usefulness of Latin American populism as a way of understanding populism in general.

Populism in Latin America

Seeing populism as a feature of Latin American politics often means stressing the relationship between the region and other parts of the international economy, emphasizing the high level of dependence of Latin American economies and on the particular feature of economic crisis (see, for example, Di Tella, 1965). For James Malloy (1977: 9), therefore, populism is 'a specific and indigenous regional response to a general crisis which emerged from the exhaustion of a particular phase of delayed dependent development'. Tying the emergence of populism to the nature of economic development is common when looking at populism in the 'Third World'. Populism in Latin America therefore had the goals of national economic independence, breaking semi-feudal structures and promoting social justice, but because it tended to rely on leadership, centralization, money and reward, populism actually ended up extending rather than restructuring the nature of politics (Malloy 1977: 11–15). Central to such contextual understandings of populism are the twin ideas that populism (and particularly populist electoral success) comes at times of particular economic crisis and that populism fails to deliver on its message of fundamental structural change because it is essentially reformist rather than revolutionary.

The analyses of populism in Latin America that stress economic factors are inherently contextual in nature. They are specific in placing populism as the result of the particular position of Latin American economies in the global economy. They are also particular in identifying the moment at which this structural position in the global economy will give rise to populism. Such analyses may be fruitful for explaining populist movements and regimes in Latin America, but they are less useful for seeing how these regimes and movements relate to other populist phenomena elsewhere.

Developing new coalitions at a local level by bringing in the excluded as new voters and campaigning to clean up and reform government was a tactic adopted in local city politics in the 1920s by a number of politicians seeking power in Rio de Janeiro in Brazil. When Getúlio Vargas created a revolution in 1930 he brought many of these figures into office, but he created a regime with great dictatorial powers centred around him. Vargas was over-thrown by the military in 1945. However, when he ran for election again in 1950 he had wholeheartedly adopted the populist mantle. He stressed that he was only reluctantly returning to politics because he was needed and portrayed himself as carried back into politics 'on the arms of the people' (Dulles 1967; Conniff 1999: 48). It is a common claim of populists to be reluctant politicians because this is a way of embodying symbolically the populist ambivalence about politics in general while at the same time actually taking part in it. Vargas won the election, promising price controls and wage increases and urging the workers to help him in combating the exploiters who were causing the high cost of living (Dulles 1967: 306). Once in office he began to deliver on his promises of econ-omic planning and the just distribution of wealth by nationalizing the major industries and by focusing on welfare and social reforms, but was defeated by the economic conditions of sharply rising levels of inflation. By 1954 a military coup led Vargas to take his own life.

Vargas illustrates how populism began to permeate Brazilian politics. He centralized and personalized power. As president between 1930 and 1945 he had shown little regard for democratic institutions and had established a new constitution giving him dic-tatorial powers. By the time he returned to politics in 1950 he sought to create new patterns of support by pursuing policies of social reform and used the democratic process to give his rule legit-imacy. What Vargas lacked was great personal charisma (Levine 1970: 13). Combining new electoral coalitions with policies of social reform and with a heavy emphasis on leadership, Vargas was a proto-populist in what was to become a Latin American tradition. That combination was made even more potent by the added flavour of truly charismatic leadership, and it was one that marked Perón's career in neighbouring Argentina.

Juan Perón and Peronism

Argentina in the 1940s was in the grip of economic crisis. The government was a conservative one that followed from the regime of the military that had installed itself through a coup in 1930 and which kept itself in power through electoral fraud. It successfully

rode the depression of the 1930s by expanding the government's
role in the economy, but the 1940s brought new difficulties with the
Second World War and with a crisis in Argentina's relationship with
the USA (Rock 1983: 214–15). In June 1943 a group of army officers
including Juan Perón seized power from the government.

It soon became apparent that Perón was a dynamic and astute
political operator. His entry into politics at this level was by no
means spontaneous as he had developed both ambitions and strategies for realizing those ambitions throughout his early life. He had
come from an unremarkable military career and had played a
minor role in the military coup of 1930. His reflections on the subsequent regime reinforced in his mind the importance of gaining
mass support. His work in the military had also taken him to Italy
in 1939, and he had observed how Mussolini's regime demonstrated
the power of the labour movement (Page 1983: 66). By the time he
and his fellow officers seized power in 1943, Perón had seen the
possibilities of seizing power by force, the need to sustain it through
garnering mass support and the scope for seeing the labour movement as a potential source of support. He had been instrumental in
secretly organizing his fellow officers prior to the coup (Crassweller
1987: 98).

With the woman who was to become his second wife, Maria Eva
Duarte ('Evita'), Perón cultivated the support of the unions and the
poor in his position as head of the Secretariat of Labour and Social
Security. He won support through his policies of wage rises, rent
freezes and the recognition of unions. Consolidating his position in
the government, he added positions as Minister of War, head of the
Post-War Council and vice-president by 1945, but this bought him
into conflict with others in the government.

Hostility grew towards the military government. Perón's fellow
army leaders eventually jailed him in October 1945, giving rise to
widespread labour protests. These culminated in a mass rally on 17
October in the Plaza de Mayo where 300,000 ensured Perón's
mythic status by clamouring for his appearance. The crowd were
only satisfied when they heard from him in person that he was free
and then they dispersed peacefully (Page 1983: 128–33). The
iconography of Perón appearing on the balcony to greet the masses
who chanted his name and greeted his appearance with an ovation
became an integral component in his subsequent rule as the symbol
of his direct link to the people and his genuine popular support.

Free elections were organized in the following year and Perón was elected president. He announced a five-year plan for industrialization and development. With Evita dispensing money to the poor through her control of charitable funds gained from pressure applied to industrialists, and with Perón dispensing a massive programme of policies of redistribution and welfare, the couple shored up their position of not only national power but also real popular support and as cultural icons. Perón consolidated his party base by creating the Single Party of the Revolution (later the Peronist Party), and made the Secretariat of Labour the only state source of collective bargaining. He ensured that the Supreme Court would not stop him in his policies by using his majority in the legislature to successfully impeach and therefore oust the non-Peronist justices (Page 1983: 165–7).

Perón won the support of the unions through his policies. This came with costs. One was that he was intolerant of independent unions, as these broke the link between labour and his administration. He therefore ensured that only unions granted union status by the government could negotiate and that only one union would be recognized per sector (Page 1983: 176). The other cost was that he did little to change the patterns of agrarian ownership in rural Argentina, and although the wealthy suffered from increased taxation under Perón they were safe from having their property confiscated.

To shore up his political power Perón began changing the Constitution in 1948. This allowed for the re-election of the president (i.e. Perón) and gave grounds for stifling dissent. He essentially curtailed freedom of speech by preventing his opponents from gaining access to radio or newspapers and by invoking the law of disrespect which made it illegal to offend public officials' dignity in the exercise of their powers (Page 1983: 209). In his treatment of political parties, Perón embodied the populist distrust of parties. He converted his own party into essentially a vehicle for himself and outlawed opposition parties when he had the chance.

Perón's regime crystallized around three rallying cries: social justice, economic freedom and political independence. They were, at the same time, both vague and yet an accurate guide to his policies. Perón began to express the social justice idea in the concept of *justicialismo*. Significantly, this concept emerged three years after he took office and was not a guiding principle so much as a rationalization of what Perón, by instinct, had been doing (Crassweller 1987: 227). Social justice was represented in his attempts to improve the conditions of the urban working class and to give them rights through those he incorporated into the Constitution. *Justicialismo* placed great weight on unity and flexibility, so allowing Perón huge range in how he applied the concept (Page 1983: 220). In this sense it is a classically populist concept.

Economic freedom embodied, in the positive sense, the idea of all being allowed to have a better life. This meant that it applied to the workers, and he delivered on this by increasing wages and holidays. But in the negative sense, economic freedom signalled that the state was not going to fundamentally alter patterns of ownership. Classically populist then, it meant something different depending on who was being addressed.

Political independence was embodied in the 'Third Position', which was the phrase that Perón used to describe his foreign policy. This, in theory, meant a 'Third Position' between the two sides of the Cold War. In practice it amounted to an attempt to placate the USA by portraying Peronism as a bulwark against communism while, at the same time, cultivating the support of the USSR through his denunciations of the excesses of capitalism (Page 1983: 185–7). The 'Third Position' was also another consequence of the flexibility and pragmatism that *justicialismo* advocated (Crassweller 1987: 228). Once again, the 'Third Position' amounted to a classically populist invocation of a concept to mean as much as it could to as many without actually amounting to that much itself.

The three public themes of Perón were supplemented by one other, which he used to think about how to achieve his ends. This was the idea of the political conductor. Politics was seen as a dynamic process requiring someone to direct it and to collaborate with the people. In the concept of the conductor, it is possible to see how Perón viewed leadership. He took the idea from the military, and it stressed a particular relationship between the leaders and led. The leader's role was to locate a mass, inculcate them with doctrine, and organize them into a structure so that they would thereby become a community with a sense of rights and duties and be capable of following the leader (Page 1983: 222–3). Leaders therefore made masses capable of being led. For Page (1983: 223) this concept 'exposes the amorality underlying Perón's approach to politics. What succeeds is good, and success justifies the mantle of leadership'. It certainly both demonstrates Perón's attitude to the masses (as essentially pliant) and explains his hostility to political parties and to the Congress (his legislature) as institutions that could only distort the relationship between the leaders and the led (Crassweller 1987: 230).

Evita died in 1952 and Perón was ousted by opposition forces in 1955. He lived in exile but was eventually re-elected president in September 1973 after his party had been successful in electing his chosen candidate as president in the elections in March 1973. This had marked the end of the rule of the military junta and allowed Perón to return to Argentina and to stand as a presidential candidate. The success of his party owed much to his ability to mobilize against the military rulers (in the first election) and then to campaign for national unity (Smith 1983). Back in office, he returned to the policies of wage increases, albeit at a more moderate level. His return was to be short-lived as he died in July 1974 from a heart attack.

Peronism as populism

Peronism was based on charismatic leadership, an agenda of social reform, a cross-class alliance of support and a tendency towards authoritarianism. Describing Peronism himself, Perón declared that

> Peronism is humanism in action . . . a doctrine of social economy under which . . . our wealth . . . may be shared out fairly among those who have contributed by their efforts to amass it . . . Peronism is not learned, nor just talked about: one feels it or else disagrees. Peronism is a question of the heart rather than of the head.
>
> (Quoted in Page 1983: 219)

His rule had secured genuine popular support for this ideology, but it had relied on force to sustain its position.

Perón's personal qualities and his ability to inspire reverence were key tools for his success in elections. Just as important was his cultivation of a cross-class alliance that won the support of the urban working class through redistributive policies but which also relied on the rural vote of the poor. He centralized power institutionally and in practice. The creation of a single Peronist party, of a single charitable foundation (run by Evita), his treatment of the Supreme Court, and his record of opposition to independent unions illustrate that he was not afraid to use his position to shore up his personal power. The populism of Perón comes down to the politics of charismatic leadership in the name of, and with the support of, the politically weak but with strong centralizing tendencies used to buttress this 'popular' rule.

Perón's period of rule in Argentina offers a useful glimpse into populism as politics in practice as a regime. The role and uses of leadership in putting Perón into power embedded his personality into the populist ideas of the regime. Leadership also offered a powerful tool for bypassing the difficulties of sustaining a truly mass populist movement of protest into power. This created its own tensions. Perón's appeal was partially built on his democratic credentials of being the embodiment of the people, and the practice of building up electoral coalitions was testimony to the power of this. That tension arose with his autocratic tendencies as well as his own mythic status as leader is because these were at odds with his status as democratic leader. Perón's experience illustrates the populist resort to charismatic leadership as a way of operating within democratic institutions while at the same time harbouring fundamental disquiet at the practices of representation as normally understood.

The invocation of a sense of crisis was key to Perón's rise and also buttressed the importance of leadership. He played on economic and political crises as a justification of his policies as they were designed to achieve stability in an era of instability. The crises also offered a justification of his own personal position at the heart of the regime as in his iconography, it was, his personal qualities that offered the only hope of continuity and stability.

In Latin America, the policies of populism always amounted to reform rather than revolution. They tended to extend existing circumstances. In creating electoral bases, Perón and Vargas wooed labour to extend their existing support. In centralizing power in the offices they held, they extended the principle of centralization already there in the political systems to greater lengths. In Perón's case, the ideology of *justicialismo* was a deliberate attempt to chart a middle way between communism and capitalism. Looking from the perspective of populist supporters rather than leaders, the very emphasis on leadership, and particularly on personalized charismatic leadership, is indicative of the desire for change but not revolution. The system does not need to be fundamentally recast for populists, but all it requires, especially in times of great crisis, are great leaders who embody the wisdom of the masses. Leadership therefore becomes a substitute for revolution.

6

Preaching Populism: Social Credit in Canada

The agrarian radicalism of the populists in the United States in the nineteenth century found a powerful echo in the Canadian province of Alberta in the 1930s. A mass movement of farmers with a radical anti-establishment economic philosophy playing on the implosion of a party system and widespread dissatisfaction gave Social Credit a powerful momentum that brought it to power in Alberta and rippled through Canadian national politics in the era. Unlike the People's Party, Social Credit's rise relied heavily on the charismatic leadership of a single individual. In that way its experience echoed the role of leadership that Perón was to play in postwar Argentina. In the source of the ideas, there is an echo of the experience of the Russian *narodniki* because the ideas were brought in from outside and used as an attempt to mobilize and legitimize the mass movement. In the history of Social Credit, we have the rise of a populist movement leading to a Social Credit government in Alberta, but a move away from populism in its ideas in practice.

The rise of Social Credit

The philosophy of social credit is an economic and moral theory designed to ameliorate the effects of capitalist depression and inflation that is underlaid by a moral philosophy about the rights of individuals. It was a theory first put forward by the Scottish engineer Clifford Douglas in the early twentieth century, and it explained the 'poverty in the midst of plenty' through the power of the financial system in the machine age.[1] Although not anti-capitalist, it saw a place for the state ownership of industry, as only through the state could the monetary system be controlled. The state would determine the just price of goods, and distribute a national dividend to every person which would be based on a survey of the real wealth of the nation and which would provide for their basic needs (Irving 1959: 5–6).

In Douglas's writings there was an indictment of the existing democratic party system as a mechanism 'to direct public attention to a profitless wrangle in regards to methods' (Douglas quoted in Macpherson 1962: 127) and away from the real choices about the goals of the economic system. The implication of this was the political theory that, for social credit to be implemented, the people should be consulted about the broad parameters of policy while experts should produce mechanisms to bring this policy about (Macpherson 1962: 128). Although not populist in the sense that this explicitly gave power to elites, and to educated elites at that, it was populist in what it left out: the politicians. Douglas's writings therefore gave rise to particular difficulties when it was politicians who had themselves elected to enact a Social Credit agenda in Canada.

Lead by William Aberhart, a former teacher and preacher, the philosophy of Social Credit was taken up in the Canadian province of Alberta during the depression in the 1930s. Aberhart used radio addresses and his considerable oratory powers to spread the Social Credit message, and began organizing study groups and public meetings in 1933 in Calgary (Irving 1959: 51–2, 58). His religious oratory and commentary on the depression combined to give his advocacy of social credit real popularity. He came to use popularizing devices to communicate the Social Credit message, such as radio plays in which a 'man from Mars' came to find out about the situation in Alberta and was enlightened about Aberhart's ideas. He projected a folksy style which could be seen in his speech and in his wearing of a patched-up coat to symbolize the attempts of established politicians to deal with the depression (Irving 1959: 339).

Conflict grew within the movement as secular leaders took a stronger role and as a line of division opened up between those who saw social credit as requiring federal action and those who saw it as feasible within Alberta. Aberhart, advocating the possibility of Alberta as a forum for social credit, was briefly usurped as head of the Social Credit movement. The new leaders attempted to use a visit by Douglas to Alberta as a forum to humiliate and thus side-line Aberhart. Douglas was also keen that social credit should be implemented at the widest possible level. Ironically, Douglas's own effect was to reinforce the importance of Aberhart to the move-ment as Douglas came across as a dull and somewhat patronizing speaker. The two figures had an argument. The new leader resigned and Aberhart, to popular acclaim, reclaimed leadership of the movement. What was significant was that in Alberta, as a result, Aberhart became effectively a greater authority on the Social Credit ideas of Douglas than Douglas himself.

Aberhart built the movement through 1934 but it remained essentially a movement of pressure. He was helped in this by con-troversies surrounding the dominant parties. Ironically the domi-nant party at the time of Social Credit was the United Farmers of Alberta (UFA) which had risen in power in Alberta since 1921 as a reaction against the prevailing party system. It was at this time embroiled in scandal, and the decline in its standing among its con-stituency meant that Social Credit could capitalize on its contrast with the UFA. Social Credit was an agrarian phenomenon, and therefore the disintegration of the principal forum for the rep-resentation of farmers was highly significant.

In moving more directly into politics, Aberhart in his broadcasts made the point that there were many honest men who had not taken part in politics because it was seen as dominated by political machines. He asked for his listeners to send in, anonymously, details of how many honest men there were in their districts and what qualities they had. Four hundred names were sent in, screened, and many ended up as candidates in the forthcoming election (Irving 1959: 112). Following that, in January 1935 Aber-hart attempted to convince the UFA to adopt Social Credit as a plank in their provincial programme. He failed.

Aberhart marshalled his movement to enter politics by standing as an independent force in the 1935 election. He was anxious that the movement not become a party because he wanted it to be seen as a crusade and as untainted by association with the corruption and treachery surrounding the established parties. He built up momen-tum for this switch in strategy through conducting a straw poll and through launching a series of conventions (Irving 1959: 123–9).

Aberhart was clearly keen that the movement should be seen to transform itself into an electoral force through pressure from below, despite his evident control of the movement's fortunes. To charges that he was a dictator, Aberhart replied: 'The Spirit of Christ has gripped me. I am only seeking to clothe, feed, and shelter starving people. If that is what you call a dictator, then I am one' (quoted in Irving 1959: 136).

The results of Aberhart's leadership were spectacular. In the 1935 election Social Credit won 56 of the 63 seats and the UFA won none. Once in office, Aberhart had great difficulty or a marked reluctance to start implementing the Social Credit programme and to wrest control from the financial institutions. He bypassed the legislature and used the radio and direct appeals to the public in lieu of the support of elected members of his own movement. Forced by a rebellion in his movement, Aberhart created a board which effectively was given huge powers, and the legislature and the Social Credit movement were effectively excluded from policy making. With the onset of the Second World War the context changed, and Social Credit was effectively excused for not breaking away from the federal government (Macpherson 1962: 202). In 1943 Aberhart died. After the war Social Credit turned its attention to opposing socialism but, by 1948, the Social Credit Board had been abolished. Social Credit remained in power in Alberta until 1971, but once in power it had quickly moved a long way from the populist policies originally advocated by Aberhart.

Social Credit as populism

Social Credit in Alberta in the 1930s combined key populist ingredients: it demonized its opponents, advocated radical reform just short of revolution, supported state intervention and revered its leader. From opposition to financial and monetary elites, it fashioned a philosophy of social and economic reform, mixing egalitarianism with a strong role for the state, and was built on the foundation of a movement fundamentally dependent on the charismatic and personalized leadership of Aberhart. It also had, in the early part of the period, a strong educational strategy which is reminiscent of the role that Alliance lecturers played in the early stages of the Populist movement in the USA. It is something of a curiosity that populism, which seeks to take its wisdom from the people, often puts much effort into educating those same people concerning their wisdom. Nonetheless,

the cultivation of study groups by Aberhart had the effect of building up the basis for his political movement. The success of the
movement and taking office gave Social Credit the difficulties of
both power and institutionalization. As an anti-party its appeal was
strong, but this limited the degree to which it could sustain itself
once Aberhart took control in Alberta.

As a case to compare with other populist movements, it is
unusual in the source of its ideas. Populism, because it seeks to root
itself in the heartland and in the people that are its natural constituency, does tend to be hostile to ideas generated from outside.
The importance of both indigenously created ideas and those ideas
being particularized by populists is most evident in the case of the
Russian *narodniki*, but it is by no means confined to them. That the
ideas of Douglas, a Scot, had such a hold over the movement and
over the politics of Alberta in the period is therefore something of
a curiosity. The key to this seems to be the leadership of Aberhart.
Aberhart's role as a leader was something akin to being an interpreter of social credit ideas. The eclipsing of Douglas as a force in
the movement demonstrates that it was Aberhart's advocacy of
Douglas's ideas that gave them such potency for the Social Credit
constituency as much as the ideas themselves.

Aberhart's status within Social Credit and his centrality to the rise
of the movement, as with Perón in Argentina, gives us an insight into
another version of leadership within populist movements. What is
distinct about Aberhart's leadership is how it illuminates the quasi-
religious tone that can emerge in populist movements. Aberhart's
background in religious teaching was by no means incidental to the
techniques he used to build the movement. It is also instructive that
his own conversion to the ideas of social credit was akin to a
religious conversion, in that it was sudden and life-transforming.
The tone, language and tenor of Aberhart's subsequent advocacy of
social credit ideas resonated with religious imagery. The followers
of Aberhart reciprocated in treating him as having unique insight
into social credit ideas, as having therefore access to esoteric knowledge, and he assumed the mantle of teacher and interpreter of the
ideas. The strong quasi-religious overtones illustrate how populists
can almost go so far as to advocate non-political ideas to solve the
crises that they see about them.

The ideas of Social Credit, as exemplified in the creation of a
board to implement its policies, were hostile to politics in general
and explicitly a rejection of representative politics. The desire to

create a technical solution to problems of social justice and the economy reveals an inherent political theory that premises itself on the essential solidarity of interests of the people and on the failure of prevailing politics to reflect that unity. Representative politics is premised on a political theory that assumes that the purpose of politics is the resolution of conflict and therefore that fundamental divisions of interests are inevitable. To advocate, as Social Credit did, the resolution of conflict by technicians is to move away from the very *raison d'être* of representative politics itself.

Social Credit was an extremely successful social movement. In government its record was more problematic. It certainly failed consistently or systematically to put the ideas of social credit into practice as a government. It was less of a failure in more narrowly populist terms as a movement of displacement of established elites by new coalitions of disgruntled and discontented citizens.

Social Credit is an exceptional case of populism because it allows us to see populism, in the one example, as a movement, as leadership (that of Aberhart), as a clear set of ideas (social credit) and the fate of all these as a regime (as Social Credit government in Alberta). As such Social Credit is an example of the success of populism as a social movement but also of the limits of implementing populist ideas.

Note

1 For a full explanation of Douglas's theories, see Macpherson (1962), especially Chapters 4, 5 and 7.

7

The New Populism

The new populism is a contemporary form of populism that emerged, primarily but not exclusively in Western Europe, in the last part of the twentieth century. It is a populism that has been advocated by a number of parties on the far right of the political spectrum as a reaction against the dominance and the agenda of certain key parties of government in their party systems, and which is usually associated with particular political leaders. Learning from the 'new politics' parties and movements of the left in the 1970s and 1980s, the new populism has combined its ideological critique of the prevailing politics with the adoption of structural forms that embody its critique of political parties. Unlike the cases of populism examined in previous pages, the new populism is not a single party or movement but rather a series of different political parties in different countries arising during the same period and character-ized by some very similar themes. The similarities and simultane-ousness are not coincidental.

For our purposes, the new populism illustrates most clearly the anti-institutional politics of populism in general. The attack on political parties, party systems, and the agendas of party politics, and new populism's appearance in different countries at the same time, clearly have something to tell us about the state of contem-porary party politics in the widest possible sense.

New populism in Western Europe

The post-war consensus that prevailed in most Western European states after the Second World War embodied the ideals of social democracy and the commitment to a mixed economy, Keynesianism and the welfare state, and extended not only from social democratic parties but also to Christian democratic and conservative and liberal parties. In addition to new parties and a new agenda, social democracy also contributed a new form of political party, the mass party, reliant on mass membership.

The first big challenge to the post-war consensus came in the form of the new social movements in the 1970s and 1980s. These movements advocated a commitment to the environment, feminism, students' rights, and opposed nuclear power and war. The movements found their party expression in the 'new politics'. These were primarily green parties but also parties of the 'new left' that merged the egalitarianism of the traditional left with a new commitment to libertarianism, opposing the extension of the state and power that occurred under the post-war consensus. These were often the first new parties to effectively enter party systems for half a century. They not only challenged the consensus between the major parties, but also amounted to a profound challenge to the centre-left, to the social democratic and labour parties. The new politics parties tugged at the constituencies of centre-left parties and attacked their agendas. They also attacked the prevailing model of political parties.

New politics parties' challenges to politics were as much associated with the style of politics as with the new politics agenda. As a way of embodying their opposition to the bureaucratized state and therefore also the highly rigid, bureaucratized and hierarchical political parties, many green parties established ways of organizing that downplayed leadership by having 'spokespersons' rather than leaders. There was a concerted effort to ensure gender balance in these positions, as an embodiment of their commitment to the new politics agenda of gender equality, and so often the leadership was collective. In an attempt to further avoid the personalization of politics, they adopted rotation as a principle so that key posts would not stay with individual figures in the party.

Following on from the wave of new politics parties on the left of the party systems, a wave of parties that were at the other end of the political spectrum achieved success. During the 1980s and 1990s, there was a surge in support for parties located on the far right of the ideological spectrum. For some, this amounted to a resurgence of fascism and a potential rerun of the inter-war years and therefore they characterized it as neo-fascism (see, for example, Cheles *et al.* 1995). What was really happening was that neo-fascism, which had become an almost perennial and extremely marginal feature of post-war party systems, was coinciding with a new wave of populism.[1] This new populism, like the new politics, reacted against the development of a heavily bureaucratized welfare state and stressed the corruption and collusion in established political parties. Like the new politics, new populism rejected the consensus of the post-war settlement, but, unlike the new politics, it sought to reconstruct politics around issues of taxation, immigration and nationalism or regionalism. Which of these is stressed by new populists depends on the national context of the parties. The combination of new populism and neo-fascism gave a real political and electoral impetus that allowed parties on the far right to make significant inroads into Western European political systems.

The new populism represents a contemporary form of populism that stems from a populist rejection of the political agenda, institutions and legitimacy of the modern welfare-state model of mixed-economy capitalism. New populism shares a rejection of the post-war consensus with the new politics and also shares the attempt to fashion new ways of organizing itself as a party as an embodiment of its rejection of the prevailing mode of politics, and particularly the dominant political parties.

New populist parties organize themselves in ways that are in contrast to those of existing parties. One of the reasons for this is that populism has an inherent distrust of political institutions in general and political parties in particular. Therefore the new populists have structured their parties so as to minimize the similarity with the dominant model of how parties are organized. This means, in practice, that there is a strong rhetorical commitment to the active and direct participation of the membership of the party. At the same time, the personalized leadership of key individuals is the other side of the coin.

Making themselves, in organizational terms, different from political parties also has the function of allowing the new populists to reinforce a crucial element in their appeal to voters. Looking distinct from the other parties implicitly echoes the message of the need for a change of politics, for moving away from the cosy and corrupt consensus of the major parties. Placing themselves ideologically outside the centre of the existing party system, new populists stress their links to the common sense of the common people and see themselves as having a special connection to the positive aspects of the way politics was previously constituted.

It is difficult to be very precise about the voters for new populism because it arises in such diverse settings and such different societies. However, there do seem to be two broad features to their constituencies. They tend to draw disproportionately on young, urban men very often employed in the private sector (Taggart 1995: 43). The second feature is that voters will be volatile, in the sense that they may well be drawn from all corners of the political spectrum (if they have voted before). They are also less likely to be loyal party identifiers, and therefore unlikely to stick with new populist parties through thick and thin. In this sense, the voters reflect the 'anti-partyness' of the parties they are drawn to vote for.

The new populism reflects a contemporary form of the anti-institutional element of populism in general. The chameleonic nature of populism means that it takes on particular salient issues of its context as both expressions of and motivations for its anti-institutionalization. In broader terms, the contemporary purchase that new populism has within a number of countries tells us something about the state of representative politics, and particularly about the party systems in those countries. New populism is not confined to Western Europe, but in the range and variation of its Western European manifestations we have the richest source from which to construct an understanding. The new populism is a reaction to certain types and tendencies of party systems within contemporary liberal democratic systems. In the agenda of the dominant parties in those systems and in the forms that representation has been embedded in those systems, new populism finds fertile ground for mobilizing small but not insignificant populations of protest.

New populist parties in Western Europe

New populism, like populism in general, takes on aspects of the environment in which it finds itself. All new populism, finding itself in bureaucratized welfare states, constructs its critique against that context. Because of the different national settings of party and political systems, different 'buttons' are pushed to try and hit on the sentiment of opposition to the systems. In welfare-rich Scandinavian states, the new populism stresses the burdens of high taxation and of liberal immigration policies. In countries with significant regional and ethnic divisions, such as Belgium, Italy and Switzerland, new populism tends to focus on regional ethnic identities. For countries with highly politicized immigration politics such as

France, Austria and Germany, the new immigrant communities become the scapegoats and the new populism draws on an explicitly racist and nationalist agenda. Looking at each of these clusters in turn, the particular experiences of new populism allow us to trace the lines of continuity with the larger concept of populism.

The French experience of new populism is embodied in the success of the Front National, which has become a symbol for the far right in Europe generally. The party's founder and guiding force is Jean-Marie Le Pen. Le Pen's past brings us into contact with France's previous populist episode, as Le Pen was elected in 1956 as a deputy for the Union de Défense des Commerçants et Artisans (UDCA). This was the party of Pierre Poujade.

Poujadism grew out of a number of local actions by shopkeepers in 1953. Combining familiar populist touchstones of opposition to taxation and government authority, a number of local shopkeepers used the technique of having large gatherings outside shops which were to be visited by tax inspectors, to prevent entry by the inspectors. This was a way of expressing their frustration at the lot of the small shopkeeper. By November 1954 the UDCA had been formed as a national movement.

Pierre Poujade emerged as the movement's leader. He embodied the movement's aspirations, and his personality and qualities were important tools in mobilizing mass support (Hoffman 1956: 32–3). Poujade cultivated an image of being one of the class he represented, using simple and direct language and speaking in shirtsleeves (Eatwell 1982: 75). The movement opposed taxation, the dominance of Paris, bureaucracy and politicians in general. By 1955, Poujade had decided to form a party, the Union et Fraternité Française (UFF), and the party won 11.6 per cent of the vote and 52 seats (including that of Le Pen) in the national elections in 1956.

The year 1956 was Poujadism's high-water mark. The party's vote dropped dramatically in subsequent elections, and it petered out due to internal conflict and the changed political environment brought about by the Algerian War. When Le Pen formed the Front National in 1972 he was effectively bringing back the legacy of populist Poujadism but combining it with a militantly nationalistic anti-immigrant message that began to find real electoral resonance among some French voters. By 1984 the party had built a reputation for militant right-wing populism and a constituency of voters that gave it 11 per cent of the votes in the elections to the European Parliament and an international prominence. By 1997 the party had established itself as an integral part of the French party system and was gaining 15 per cent of the vote in both presidential and parliamentary elections.

The personality, leadership and style of Le Pen were key to the success of the party. Le Pen led the party in a highly authoritarian manner, concentrating power on himself. His image as a bombastic larger-than-life figure ensured the compliance of his party because of its electoral success. Le Pen's hold over the party was damaged after a near putsch by his deputy Bruno Megret led to the party dividing into two distinct parts. Although no longer unequivocally leader of the far right in France, Le Pen's figure looms large over the rise of the National Front and therefore over the far right in Europe more generally. The party's electoral record, one of the best for the far right in Western Europe, owed much to the combination of neofascism with new populism and demonstrated the potential for parties of the far right to establish themselves within party systems.

Another extremely prominent figure of the European far right is Jörg Haider in Austria. He achieved notoriety by making statements that suggested his support for Hitler's employment policies, but the secret of his success was in his sustained critique of the Austrian political system combined with a heavy streak of xenophobia. In 1986 Haider became leader of the Austrian Freedom Party (FPÖ), a party that historically was representative of the liberal and nationalist section of Austrian society (Luther 1992: 47). By 1994 the Freedom Party had gained 22.5 per cent of the national vote, but it had done so with a new and very different agenda.

Austrian politics in the post-war period saw the dominance of the social democrats (SPÖ) and the conservatives (ÖVP). The two parties governed together as a 'Grand Coalition' and, when not sharing power, effectively alternated in office. This allowed the Freedom Party to portray the other parties as a cartel excluding other parties from power. Haider capitalized, on this. The Freedom Party began to combine its protest character with an agenda of economic freedom, privatization, emphasis on traditional family values and vehement opposition to immigration (Riedlsperger 1998: 31–4). The combination has been a powerful one, giving the Freedom Party electoral success and bringing it into position as the second biggest party in the Austrian parliament in the 1999 national elections. In February 2000, the party entered government as part of a coalition with the conservatives, giving rise to vociferous domestic and international protest.

Haider's populism came out not only in the agenda of the Freedom Party but also in his attempt to buttress the party's agenda with direct democratic initiatives. In 1992 he attempted to mobilize a referendum campaign for tough immigration laws. In 1994 he mobilized against Austria's membership of the EU in the national referendum. In both cases he found himself and his party on the losing side, but it is significant that the direct democratic tool of the referendum was a natural focus for Haider's new populism. Parties are tainted institutions for new populists but also insufficient for new populist mobilization, and so it is natural to seek alternative ways of winning support.

Any attention to the far right in Europe inevitably leads to a consideration of the German case. The Nazi legacy has meant that observers, politicians and citizens (both in and outside Germany) have been particularly sensitive to far right activity. In fact, Germany has not seen a great amount of new populist mobilization. Parties of the far right have been electorally relatively unsuccessful. The Republikaner attained at best 2.1 per cent of the vote in national elections in 1990, although there are regional variations and they have been more successful when contesting European Parliament elections.

The Republikaner have been associated with the leadership of Franz Schönhuber, who led the party between 1985 and 1994. Under his tenure the party developed its profile of being suspicious of immigration, critical of crime, for the family, for lowered taxes and for a 'healthy patriotism' (Winkler and Schumann, 1998: 103). Given the constraints of the German Basic Law which requires all parties to adhere to support for the democratic system, the party was very careful not to be seen to be acting unconstitutionally.

In Scandinavia, the traditional dominance of social democratic parties meant that the welfare state was developed to a higher degree than elsewhere. The benefit of this was that it fostered an atmosphere of social consensus when economic growth was good. When economic hard times were encountered the costs of high taxation associated with generous welfare provision were much more likely to be the object of attention. Taxation has become the lever with which new populist parties in Scandinavia have attempted to prise voters away from social democratic parties and from the political and social consensus associated with centre-left social welfare politics.

The emergence of the Progress Party in Denmark was relatively spectacular. Based on the leadership of Mogens Glistrup, the Progress Party broke through in 1973 on a platform of abolishing income tax, cutting bureaucracy and deregulation (Svåsand 1998: 82). It gained its highest ever share of the vote (15.9 per cent) at that election. Since then, although Glistrup left the party in 1990 to be replaced as leader by Pia Kjærsgaard, the party has remained as a small but not insignificant party in the Danish party system with a consistent electoral record (Andersen 1992). The party initially depended heavily of the style and agenda of Glistrup. It was only in the late 1980s that anti-immigration was added to the party's stance.

At the same time as Glistrup's initial success in Denmark, Anders Lange was establishing a new party in Norway. Although lacking the spectacular start that the Danish party had, Lange's party became the Progress Party and, after his death in 1974, was led by Carl Hagen. Like its Danish counterpart, Progress became an established party in the Norwegian party system, gaining 15.2 per cent of the vote in 1997 elections. It advocated reducing the size of the public sector, opposed Norwegian entry in the European Union and called for a reduction in the rate of immigration (Svåsand 1998: 83–4).

In 1991 a new party was formed in Sweden by two colourful public figures, a businessman and author Ian Wachtmeister and Bert Karlsson, the owner of a fun-fair. The party was called New Democracy and campaigned on issues of reducing taxation, cutting immigration and liberalizing alcohol laws (Taggart 1996: 6–7). The style of the party was deliberately irreverent (a 'smiley' face was the party logo), the rhetoric was both colourful and bombastic, and the target was invariably the complacency and inefficiency of the established political class. Leadership was vital to the party, and it organized itself self-consciously in a way that minimized its bureaucratic structure while maximizing the degree of freedom for the leadership. The party's rhetoric stressed the impact of the ordinary party members on the party's policies (Taggart 1996: 121–9).

New Democracy's electoral success was limited: it gained 6.7 per cent of the vote in the 1991 election, but by 1994 it had slumped to only 1.8 per cent. In-fighting within the party and the loss of Wachtmeister weakened the party's position. In addition, the party's support for the government after 1991 meant that it had difficulty in sustaining its image and appeal as the *enfant terrible* of the Swedish party system. After the 1994 election the party effectively disappeared. Although unsuccessful, New Democracy, in its brief life, did reflect new populism in Sweden.

Looking at the way that new populism has appeared in other Western European countries, the issue of regional, national and ethnic identities comes to the fore. This seems to be the case in countries with significant regional divisions. In Italy the long-established distinction between the North and the South has allowed new populism to draw on the resentment of the Northerners to the alleged benefits that have been given to the economically poorer South.

The identity and claims of Northerners were crystallized into the demands of the Northern League (Lega Nord) which argued that parts of Northern Italy constitute an area with real cultural and economic identity and therefore called for secession from Rome. Like other new populist parties, it is important to recognize that the claims stem in part from the idea that somehow those who have traditionally been treated as underprivileged have become overprivileged and thus the majority is placed in an invidious situation. New populists see the need to redress the balance back towards those who have been portrayed as overprivileged but are in reality now underprivileged.

The party was led by Umberto Bossi who formed the party in the early 1980s out of a number of regional leagues. By 1992 the Northern League had won 8.7 per cent of the vote. Bossi stressed his opposition to the established political elites, his distrust of the networks of politics that seemed to tie political favours to supporters of the main parties, and the need for Northern Italy to be allowed to realize its potential as an economically successful and sustainable region. The message fell on fertile ground because the issue of corruption seemed to be threatening to engulf the Italian political system at this time.

The rise of the Northern League was interrupted by what was effectively a revolution in the Italian party system. In 1994 the dominance of the Christian democrats crumbled under the attack of wholly new forces. A powerful new force alongside the Northern League came in the shape of the media magnate Silvio Berlusconi, with Forza Italia. The dilemma that Berlusconi posed for Bossi was that Berlusconi represented a similarly new populist force. Modelling its organization on football clubs rather than on political parties, and wholly dependent on both the leadership and funding provided by Berlusconi, Forza Italia campaigned on a platform of the need to clean up Italian politics and to bring in an outsider like Berlusconi to put politics back in touch with the common people and away from the feather-bedded political class (McCarthy 1996: 43–6; Seisselberg 1996: 727–30).

Forza Italia won the largest share of the vote in the 1994 election and this put it into power. Given the short time (a matter of months) in which Forza Italia had grown up and the previous resilience of the political system to change, this feat was spectacular. Bossi had to decide whether to form a coalition with Berlusconi. This highlighted the dilemma for new populists because, while their appeal is partly based on protest, becoming part of a political establishment gives them access to power but denies them the support of those in their constituency whose allegiance is based primarily on oppositional antagonism to politics in general. In addition, Bossi had to face the strategic dilemma of going into coalition with a party which was essentially tapping the same ideological and electoral vein.

The second problem was that a resurgence on the right had breathed new life into the party on the far right of the Italian party system, the Italian Social Movement (MSI). This party is the heir to the fascist tradition in Italy. In 1994, under the leadership of Gianfranco Fini, the party moved towards a new, more palatable position. Changing its identity as the National Alliance, the party then won 13.5 per cent of the vote and a place in the governing coalition (Ignazi 1996: 703–4). The presence of such a party in government meant that Bossi had to deal with a pretender to his new populist throne from Berlusconi and the association with a neo-fascist party at the same time. Despite these difficulties, Bossi joined the coalition.

By 1996 the coalition had fractured and the left, in a new coalition, gained the government. Berlusconi himself became embroiled in charges of the very corruption he had campaigned against. The conflict within the coalition was profoundly disruptive and the Northern League was eventually instrumental in bringing the government down (Newell and Bull 1997: 98). Conflict between Berlusconi and Bossi reflected the type of conflict that is usually confined to the internal life of new populist parties. Having two new populist parties, it is possible to see a different manifestation of what seems to be a widespread feature of new populism, that of a tendency towards internal conflict over leadership and often to profound factionalism.

In Belgium the new populism played heavily on the ethnic and linguistic divide that runs through the country. Vlaams Blok (Flemish Bloc) was formed in 1978 and served as a lightning rod for Flemish nationalism. Support from the voters came from identification with the party's four main issues: opposition to immigration, hostility to the established parties and their 'corruption' and the demand for an independent Flanders (Swyngedouw 1998: 62–3). An initial focus on the issues of Flemish independence then shifted towards a much more vociferously anti-immigrant position (Husbands 1992: 137–8). The anti-immigrant issue combined with Flemish nationalism allowed the party to achieve 12.5 per cent of the vote in Flanders in 1995.

Vlaams Blok has not been dominated by charismatic leadership to the same degree as other new populist parties. It was led until 1996 by Karel Dillen whose influence was important, and, like the other parties, it developed a highly centralized structure that has ensured that the party was been both unified and under strong direction from the top (Swyngedouw 1998: 61–2).

Switzerland is another famously divided society. Powerful cultural and linguistic distinctions between the cantons mean that the political forces making up the new populism are themselves what Gentile and Kriesi (1998) call a 'divided family'. In the Italian-speaking part of Switzerland the Lega dei Ticinesi was formed in 1991. The Lega established itself as an anti-establishment party and did well in its canton, gaining up to 23 per cent of the vote. It was led by Flavio Maspoli and Giuliano Bignasca, both of them popular and charismatic. Its significance is enhanced by the concurrent rise of two other parties on the Swiss extreme right. On the one hand there was the Automobilists Party, which was founded in 1985 as a reaction against socialist and ecological parties' successes. It was an amalgam of anti-immigrant nationalism and hostility to state intervention in economic or environmental issues which has achieved up to 5.1 per cent of the national vote. On the other hand, there were the Swiss Democrats (formerly National Action), created in 1969 out of an initiative to limit the number of foreign workers in Switzerland, which established a strong anti-immigrant identity for itself.

The agenda of new populism has not been confined to Western Europe. There are other regions in which the politics of welfare-state capitalism and party consensus has featured. Hostility to parties, party systems and the agenda of politics on the part of protest voters on the right has been a fruitful path for politicians in Australia, Canada and the USA.

New populism in Australia, Canada and the United States

In 1996 a former fish and chip shop owner in Australia, Pauline Hanson, was dropped by her party, the Liberal Party, because of outspoken comments in which she attacked Aboriginal rights, the idea of multiculturalism and the phenomenon of Asian immigration. She stood as an independent in the 1996 federal election and, after having gained prominence in the media for her comments, Hanson formed her own party, One Nation, in 1997 (Johnson 1998).

Hanson's agenda subsequently embraced three key themes. On economic policy she argued for protectionism as a defence against globalization and as a way of sustaining employment. Culturally, she argued for the rights of Anglo-Celtic Australians and suggested that the agenda of multiculturalism had disadvantaged those who were in the majority and those minorities that had assimilated. This meant an attack on the privileging of Aboriginal rights. It also meant an anti-immigrant stance where she suggested that the influx of immigration from Asia was transforming Australian society. The final element was the anti-elitism that Hanson espoused. She suggested that cosmopolitan elites had sold out to special interests. The usual populist litany of politicians, bureaucrats and intellectuals was the object of her wrath. Hanson herself says:

> I may only be a 'fish and chip shop lady', but some of these economists need to get their heads out of the textbooks and get a job in the real world. I would not even let one of them handle my grocery shopping.
> (Quoted in Johnson 1998: 217)

Hanson's new populism fits the anti-immigrant cluster of new populism. The importance of both the agenda of multiculturalism and the importance of immigration in Australian history mean that Hanson's choice of target hit home in her political environment.

Canadian politics had already been rocked by a regionally based party with populist overtones in the twentieth century when Social Credit rose to power in Alberta in the 1930s (see Chapter 6). The pattern was repeated in the 1990s. Formed in 1987, the Reform Party, led by Preston Manning, returned to some of the themes of Social Credit and gained a powerful electoral foothold. The connection between Social Credit and the Reform Party was not merely ideological, as Preston Manning was the son of Ernest Manning who had succeeded Aberhart as Social Credit premier in Alberta in 1943. By 1993 the Reform Party had gained 52 seats in the national legislature. As such it was two seats short of becoming the official opposition. The party polled 19 per cent of the national vote and in the western provinces it did even better, garnering 52 per cent of the vote in Alberta (LeDuc 1994: 167). By 1997, the party edged above that hurdle with 60 seats.

The appeal of the Reform Party was based on a critique of the Canadian party system and of political elites as colluding in creating a political system that excluded ordinary people. Unlike Social Credit, the Reform Party did not demonize financial institutions but rather saw the growth of the state as unnecessarily impeding the effective functioning of market relations. Its enemies were therefore special interests and the old political class with its privileged access to government (Laycock 1994: 217).

Reform Party proposals included the introduction of referendums as an addition to the functioning of democracy and as the embodiment of the party's commitment to direct democracy (Laycock 1994: 240–3). This is seen as necessary because suffusing the party's ideology was the sense that representative democracy in Canada has overrepresented certain interests and therefore is teetering towards an overload of demands (Laycock 1994: 218).

The Reform Party's critique of politics reflects a reaction to emergence of the bureaucratized welfare state. In this sense it has not only similarities with its forebears in Social Credit but also strong similarities with the protest parties of the far right in Western Europe that emerged in the 1980s. Reform can be seen as part of the wave of new populism.

Another example of a contemporary populist party that has arisen on the back of a critique of the party system is the other Reform Party, that of Ross Perot in the United States. I have already described Perot, in Chapter 2, as the latest appearance of populism in the United States and explained him in those terms, but it is also possible to see Perot, in a wider context, as part of the new populism. Perot's initial appeal as a presidential candidate was very much on the basis of the failure of the existing party system, of the Democrats and Republicans, to provide real solutions to the growing problem of the budget deficit and the capture of US politics by special and moneyed interests.

The particular agendas of new populist parties in non-European settings vary in content from those in Western Europe, but what is still apparent is that all these parties have constituted themselves on the basis of fundamental critiques of the party systems in their countries. They share a similar populist tone and their emergence at the same time as the new populists in Western Europe may well indicate some real difficulties with liberal democracy in advanced welfare-state systems. In both the USA and Canada, the parties have had a populist heritage to draw upon and can therefore also be seen as the latest incarnations of particular populist traditions, but this should not obscure the underlying commonality of new populism in contemporary politics in different parts of the world.

I have used the 'new' in 'new populism' to emphasize the common roots of protest with the 'new politics' parties of the libertarian left. What unites these parties is the way that they organize, their broad anti-institutional ideology and their location on the far right of the ideological spectrum. What is common to the contexts that give rise to them is that these are developed welfare states with liberal democratic polities with stable party systems. The 'new-ness' of the new populism therefore is an example of the chameleonic character of populism in general.

The variation in the different forms that the new populism has taken is predominantly linked to the different types of issues that they use to mobilize support. This explains why there have been so many different approaches to these parties as they are collectively multifaceted in their issue agenda. Immigration, regionalism and taxation are stressed to varying degrees depending on the national context. This is what we would expect if they are populist because it is this aspect that makes them chameleonic, taking on the colours that are around them in terms of the lines of political debate that characterize their national social and political contexts.

At heart, new populism is an attack on the nature of political parties, and therefore on the form that representative politics has come to take in the countries in which it arises. In both the form that they take and in the positions they adopt, new populists embody a radical critique of existing parties. Organizationally they deliberately construct themselves in ways that do not resemble the established parties. New populists use divisive issues as a crowbar to lever themselves away from what they see as the cosy consensus at the heart of the party system, thereby differentiating themselves and maximizing support for their parties from voters who feel alienated from politics in general.

What unites the new populist parties is an extreme reaction to the party systems in which they find themselves and to the form that political parties are taking. This is linked to a convergence in the political agenda. In Western Europe, this convergence has been around the post-war settlement and its collapse, and, perhaps more importantly, the configuration of politics and political institutions in response to that collapse. This convergence of agenda has closed down the party systems in favour of the established mass parties usually of the centre-left or centre-right, but it has also opened up these systems to the possibility of corruption and to the certainty of the accusation of corruption (Hayward 1996; Hine 1996; Mény 1998). This is grist to the populist mill, and the new populists have not missed this opportunity to use the issue of elite corruption to shore up their support.

The self-limitation of populism is clearly visible within the new populism. As it is fundamentally anti-institutional in its orientation, it is logical that it should be particularly susceptible to the institutional dilemmas of populism. One of the features clearly visible in the fate of new populism lies in the internal life of parties. Factionalism and particularly conflict over leadership seem almost endemic to these parties. Conflict over leadership is likely as charismatic leadership becomes a replacement for the more bureaucratic institutions of representation of the mass party model. The Republikaner in Germany experienced a damaging conflict over Schönhuber's leadership. In Denmark, Mogens Glistrup saw his party effectively push him out under the leadership of Kjærsgaard. In Sweden the leadership of Wachtmeister and his differences with Karlsson led to both factionalism and eventually to the party's demise with the departure of Wachtmeister. Even Le Pen's hold on the French Front National was subject to a divisive and damaging challenge from within as Megret attempted to establish himself as leader of the far right in 1998 and 1999. While some new populist parties seem able to overcome the problems associated with a highly personalized leadership structure, it appears to be a problem that all new populist parties have had to wrestle with.

Where new populism achieved great success, in Italy, the infighting between Bossi and Berlusconi played a key role in undermining its position in government. This is hardly surprising, for achievement of government can raise a fundamental difficulty for populists. Having achieved power on the basis of their appeal as outsiders and opponents of politicians, they have to struggle to sustain that support while at the same time becoming insiders and professional politicians themselves.

New populism allows us the clearest view of the anti-institutional predisposition of populism. Looking at such a wide and, in some aspects, divergent set of examples, what shines through in this populism is a rejection of political parties and their form. The new populists are telling indicators that the agents of representative politics, parties, are in difficulties in many liberal democracies. Political parties are in a process of transformation away from the mass party model. At the same time, there is evidence that citizen attitudes towards politics in many liberal democracies are becoming more alienated and negative. The difficulty is that the populist answer is the rejection of parties and therefore a rejection of the importance of political association and therefore of representative politics. This creates problems for itself and does not provide a solution for representative politics other than to advocate its removal. The presence of new populism indicates problems with parties, but its own inherent ambivalence towards parties and the difficulties that new populism has in practically adopting but ideologically rejecting the party form, means that new populists do not offer a solution to these problems.

Note

1 There is a plethora of terms for and definitions of this new wave. I have termed it the new populism (Taggart 1995; 1996) while Immerfall (1998) similarly refers to it as 'neo-populism'. Betz (1994, 1998) refers to 'radical right-wing populists'. Ignazi (1992) speaks of the 'new right-wing parties'. Kitschelt (1995) and Merkl and Weinberg (1993) write about the 'contemporary radical right'. Others prefer to use an umbrella term that captures the full range of the far right such as the 'extreme right' (Hainsworth 1992; Harris 1990), while others are specifically concerned with those parties that only represent the resurgence of fascism and therefore focus on 'neo-fascism' (Cheles *et al.* 1995).

The Characteristics of Populism

PART TWO
The Characteristics
of Populism

8

Populism, the People and the Heartland

Populists celebrate 'the people,' especially in so far as their values contrast with those of elites. Some take the commitment to 'the people' as *the* defining feature of populism. Certainly, one of the most common features of populism is the assertion that it is for the people. It is from this position that populism derives its anti-elitism. However, we must ask ourselves what is meant by this commitment to 'the people'. Answering this question reveals that populism's rhetorical commitment to 'the people' is real in the sense that it embodies some key components of populist thinking but that the conception of 'the people' is complicated and is, at least partially, derived from populism's commitment to other concepts.

Populism and the people

Some commentators have taken populists at their own word and define populism as a movement that represents 'the people' (Westlind 1996: 99). Others take a more specific view and define populism in relation to particular social classes (e.g. Di Tella 1965; Conway 1978). In the case of Latin American populism, it is clear that the participation of the urban working classes through the labour movement was a key to their electoral success. However, as soon as we move the context of populism we move the particular class to which it seems to apply: the Russian peasantry, North American farmers and agricultural workers, the Argentinian urban working class, or the Western European urban working class employed in the private sector. Clearly, each populism may have a particular class basis, but populism does not itself have a class basis (Laclau 1977: 145). To see populism as class-based is to succumb to tying populism in general too closely to any one of the contexts in which it manifests itself.

Why are 'the people' such apparently essential ingredients in the populist equation? A simple answer is that 'the people' is an idea that is as ductile or flexible as populism needs it to be. Populism requires devices that are themselves malleable, and 'the people' is just such a device. But to say that the idea of 'the people' is invoked because of its flexibility does not necessarily mean that the idea is without meaning. It is no coincidence that the same rhetorical device is used by different populist movements. There is a core or 'heart' to the populist invocation of the people, but we need to separate this core from the way it is extended in the different practices of populism.

In untangling populism from 'the people' a useful starting point is to see what it is about 'the people' as an idea that makes them so attractive to populists. 'The people' are populist objects because of *who* they are, *who* they are *not*, *how* they are, and *how many* they are.

A key aspect of 'the people' is their number. The use of the term implies that the people are numerous and in the majority. This has a practical use – 'they' are numerous so confer greater legitimacy on those who speak in their name and provide a potential constituency who, if wholly won over, can overwhelm whatever forces are ranged against them. While the numerousness of the people is important for populists, that should not be confused with plurality or variety. The populist conception of 'the people' is as fundamentally monolithic. 'The people' are portrayed as a unity. They are seen as a single entity devoid of fundamental divisions and unified and solidaristic. 'The people' are, in populist thinking, already fully formed and self-aware. It is this feature that makes them such easy subjects. Reference to 'the people' is easily made and readily understood.

We also see populists speaking the name of 'the people' because of who they are. In this case populism draws from 'the people' because, as Margaret Canovan (1999: 5) puts it, this 'is the appeal to *our people*, often in the sense of our kith and kin'. 'The people' are celebrated because they embody certain virtues. Looking at how 'the people' are invoked in populist rhetoric, it is possible to make out a sense of 'the people' as embodying certain characteristics.

The 'silent majority' has been a theme in recent North American populist discourse and serves as a useful guide to populists elsewhere and their claim to speak for 'the people'. The notion of 'silent majority' invokes certain attributes of 'the people' that give them the claim to be heard over the clamouring minority. Part of this claim is admittedly their very silence. The implication is that silence accords with their virtue. The silence of the majority comes from the fact that they are working, paying taxes and quietly getting on with life. This means they are civic and productive but politically quiescent. With no natural inclination to become involved with the minority (elite) pursuit of politics, it is the mass citizenry who represent the heart of the population and indeed perhaps the very soul of the country. In US terms, the reference to 'Middle America' typifies this by specifying a mythical geographical location where these folks live. Politicians, as long as they have Middle America as their constituency, have the right to continue to act as representatives. Once the link is broken, then the silent majority need to act and to reassert themselves.

The link between the silent majority and their representatives is, in populist discourse, broken by two connected problems. The first is that the corruption of politics is likely to lead to the corruption of politicians, and if this process is framed within a wider context of social decay and moral collapse it is almost inevitable that this should be the fate of politicians. Populists of the right will often stress this problem because their conservatism is more likely to lead them to identify a mood of moral and social collapse as the cause of the diversion away from their favoured values inherent in the wisdom of the past and away from the sources of stability and order.

The other problem that will break the link between the politicians and their silent majority is where 'special interests' are seen to have captured the political process. For populists of the left these special interests will usually be the economic giants such as large corporations. For the Populist movement in the United States, bankers, industrialists and railroad companies constituted privileged special interests. For populists of the right, the special interests are more likely to be 'minority' groups who make claims for special rights. Those groups may be immigrants, the unemployed, environmentalists or feminists. Whatever the 'minority' groups, they are linked as being outside the 'mainstream' of politics.

The implication of mobilizing the silent majority is that the majority is reluctantly political and only shaken from that reluctance by a sense of necessity brought on by extreme conditions – by a sense of crisis or collapse. Once this army of reluctant citizens is on the move, their claims to power, according to populists, are greater than those of others because of who they are. The lack of political ambition gives greater weight to their politicization when it does happen. Their years of silent, civic consent also give them greater weight. They have earned a hearing because their voice has been silent for so long, and it is in that silence that they have proved the productive heart of the nation.

In practice, populists are often more sure of who they are not than of who they are. The demonization of social groups, and particularly the antipathy towards the elite, provides populists with an enemy, but it is also a crucial component of the attempt to construct an identity. The new populism is a very conspicuous attempt to fashion an identity for what is otherwise an amorphous and heterogeneous mass, by singling out particular social groups, be they immigrants, unemployed, or members of an opposing regional or ethnic group, and defining the new populist constituency in terms of who is excluded. There is nothing new in this. Rather it is indicative of a tendency among populists to define themselves through portraying themselves in opposition to social groups they characterize as unpleasant. The language of populist rhetoric is full of negative, demonizing imagery of pointy-headed intellectuals, bureaucrats, hacks, fat cats, robber barons, beatniks and plutocrats.

The demonization of social groups by populists has two effects. Firstly, it rallies support for those sharing a grievance against the demonized groups. In other words, it brings more support to the populist fold. Secondly, it reinforces (or even creates) a sense of solidarity among those who demonize the groups. In the absence of other bonds between supporters of populism, this second effect can be particularly important. Together these effects create enemies and solidarity.

We should be careful not to portray 'the people' as an entirely negatively constructed idea. For populists 'the people' do embody some identifiable qualities. As Wiles (1969: 166) defines it, a major premise of populism is that 'virtue resides in the simple people, who are the overwhelming majority, and in their collective traditions'. It is because of their ordinariness and their decency that 'the people' have the right to prevail. These qualities are usually used in a way that contrasts them to the corruption and the stupidity of elites. Populists see wisdom as residing in the common people. From common people comes common sense, and this is better than bookish knowledge.

There is another way of understanding the populist invocation of 'the people'. This is to understand 'the people' by *where* they are. So far, we have considered populism by taking populists at their word, looking at the language and concepts that they themselves use to evoke images and to provoke their enemies. Looking beyond and (perhaps) behind the language of populists, it is possible to trace lines of continuity between the different 'peoples' called on. This continuity lies in the heartland as the location of 'the people'.

The politics of the heartland

Populist rhetoric uses the language of the people not because this expresses deeply rooted democratic convictions about the sovereignty of the masses, but because 'the people' are the occupants of the heartland and this is what, in essence, populists are trying to evoke. As we have seen, while there is some depth to what is meant by 'the people', there is too much variation for such a notion to serve as a guiding principle of populism. The invocation of 'the people' as a rhetorical device is ubiquitous in populism because it is derivative of the deeply embedded, if implicit, conception of the heartland in which, in the populist imagination, a virtuous and unified population resides.

The heartland is a territory of the imagination. Its explicit invocation occurs only at times of difficulty, and the process yields a notion that is unfocused and yet very powerful as an evocation of that life and those qualities worth defending, thereby stirring populists into political action. The heartland is that place, embodying the positive aspects of everyday life.

Ideologies have ideal societies. Ideal societies are usually those forward projections by ideologues of the world as it would be constructed if it embodied the key values that they advocate. Sometimes these ideal worlds might constitute utopias (Levitas 1990; Kumar 1991). The heartland is different from ideal societies or utopias because it sees populists casting their imaginative glances backwards in an attempt to construct what has been lost by the present. Whereas ideal societies and, even more, utopias are constructions of the mind and the head, heartlands owe their power to the heart, to the evocation of sentiments that may not be necessarily either rationalized or rationalizable.

The invocation of the heartland accounts for another common comment about populism. Although in practice tied to the support of particular classes, populism is often seen to be in theory above class and even classless. Implied in the emphasis on 'the people' is buried the idea that these people are an undifferentiated mass. It is through their very collectiveness that they are able to produce wisdom. The singularity of the heartland implies a singularity in its population. The heartland as a single territory of the imagination demands a single populace. The unity and the homogeneity of the imaginary residents of the heartland explains why populist rhetoric is usually so geared towards seeing 'the people' as homogeneous.

The heartland is constructed not only with reference to the past, but also through the establishment of its frontiers. Put more simply, the heartland is made as a justification for the exclusion of the demonized. While the lines of inclusion are fuzzy, populists are usually much clearer about the lines of exclusion. The tendency for populists to be explicit in excluding certain groups as not part of the real 'people' finds a strong echo in the conception of the heartland. Part of this conception is that the heartland is part of that territory which is part of the national (or potentially other type of) identity but that it is a purer part of that identity. Central to the idea of the heartland is its very centrality. The heartland lies at the core of the community and excludes the marginal or the extreme. Populists see themselves as at the centre of the things, or the very heart of things.

The importance of the heartland accounts for the inward-looking nature of populism. Internationalism and cosmopolitanism are anathema to populists. The attitude to those concerns outside the boundaries of the populists' chosen people is diffident. Isolationism and insularity are the natural predispositions of populists. This is why populism has been associated with ethical nationalism (in the case of new populism), and with isolationism in terms of foreign policy (in the case of twentieth-century populism in the USA). Ideas and concerns that come from outside the heartland are very much secondary concerns for populists, if they are of interest at all. This has the effect of reinforcing the sense of unity of the heartland because it strengthens the border around this territory of the imagination.

It might be tempting to draw this inward-looking aspect of the populist heartland in terms of the nationalism, but it is important to be clear that they are distinct concepts and that attachment to either of them can have very different consequences. While populism

excludes those outside the nation, it does not include all those in the
nation. The heartland, in so far as it refers to a nation, is a very qualified nationalism, explicitly excluding a series of social groups. It is
based around the idea of an organic community that has some
natural solidarity and therefore is more circumscribed than the sort
of community contained within national boundaries. Populism will
identify with nationalism when nationalism is an expression of the
values of the heartland, but it is clear that the commitment to nation
derives from the heartland, and not vice versa.

How do we see the heartland in the politics of populism? One
way we see it is through the way 'the people' are invoked and
through the characteristics attributed to them by populists. In this
way, we can only see the heartland indirectly. Occasionally it is
directly visible in the rhetoric of populism. In the USA, the use of
'Middle America' is the explicit invocation of an American heartland. There is an echo of this in the way that 'Middle England' is
used in English politics as a reference to an imagined constituency
of the moderate mainstream heartland of England. As with Middle
America, it conjures up a romanticized ordinariness that invokes a
core constituency for the centre-ground politics of 'common sense'.

The Russian *narodniki* had a very explicit conception of the
heartland. They took what they saw as the heart of rural Russian
life and, writ large, made it into a celebrated form of life and a
model for social transformation. The peasantry, their values and
the organization of their life and politics became almost revered
icons for the Russian populists. In their celebration of the
obshchina, the *narodniki* gave more detail to their heartland than
other conceptions.

We have seen why populism invokes itself and mobilizes itself
politically at times in the name of the people. The ordinariness of
the people and the distrust of institutions are also visible in the way
that populists mobilize and what they advocate. Straightforward-
ness, simplicity and clarity are the clarion calls for populism. Populism attempts to advocate common-sense solutions in ways that are
commonly understood.

The ways of the hearth and home resonate throughout the language and the style of populists. The power of these symbols is connected to the populist celebration of 'the people' as ordinary and as
being essentially virtuous. As a way of gaining support, it is useful
to invoke such a constituency. However, part of their very virtue for
populists lies in the fact that they are not usually politically active.

Populists have therefore had to find means of mobilizing their constituencies. One of these methods has been to educate the people into activity. The difficulty in this is that it reveals a tension for populists associated with the process of mobilization. Having to be active in leading, educating and mobilizing the people means, at least in some sense, that the will of the people is being brought about from above rather than from below.

The association of populism with 'the people' is a potential dead end. It is simply too broad to tell us anything substantial about the real nature of the populist constituency, and yet for populists it is a powerful tool with great symbolic resonance. It serves populists well by mobilizing what might otherwise be diffuse interests. At the same time, constant reference to 'the people' allows populists to reinforce their democratic credentials while allowing them to reject the particular democratic politics of representation. It is a powerful idea because it plays on the tension in democracy between the power of popular sovereignty and the possibility of a tyranny of the majority.

The heartland provides us with a tool for making sense of the populist invocation of 'the people'. The populist claim to speak in the name of this constituency is not empty. It has a certain set of meanings for populists. Unfortunately the dominance of democratic ideas and the associated importance of popular sovereignty mean that the term 'the people' is used so widely and with such variation in meaning, that it is effectively robbed of meaning and certainly detatched from the specific meaning given to it by populists. It is for this reason that I suggest that, in each case of populism, it is useful to conceive of a heartland. This becomes a device through which we can detect what it is in 'the people' that populists celebrate and therefore the source of the populist commitment to 'the people'. The concept of the heartland allows us to see the commonality across different manifestations of populism, while at the same time allowing each instance of populism to construct its own particular version of the heartland.

9

Institutional Dilemmas of Populism

The instinctive, almost primal appeal of populism for its adherents gives populist movements great dynamism and momentum and a certain spectacular quality. This is particularly true of populist movements early in their existence. The costs of this are felt in the longer term. For any political movement to sustain itself for a period of time (which we must assume it should want to do because it will invariably take time to achieve its goals), it has to address the issue of how to organize itself, how to institutionalize itself. The sense of spontaneousness that often characterizes populist movements makes this process difficult, as it is problematic to sustain both an air of spontaneity and institutionalize at the same time.

Populism is, in its political expression, usually a short-lived phenomenon. This is because its attitude towards institutions creates a set of dilemmas for it that make it self-limiting. Populism contains within itself its own limits to growth. These limits are set by the problematic relationship between populism and institutions.

Political parties are key political institutions in the process of representative politics and are thus both an object of criticism and a way of mobilizing support for populists. This can create specific problems and also illustrates a fundamental institutional dilemma that faces populism. Its reaction against the institutions of representative politics is an important driving force for it, and yet, for that force to go anywhere, populism invariably has to use those institutions itself. Parties are an inherent part of representative politics and so populism is predisposed to distrust them, but it is forced to use them.

We do not have to look far to see the populist antipathy towards parties. The meteoric rise of the Social Credit Party in the Canadian province of Alberta in the 1930s owed as much to the collapse of faith in the existing parties as it did to the evangelistic zeal of its leader, William Aberhart. Although it was a party, it was anxious to avoid the use of the term in its self-description, preferring to be plain 'Social Credit' or the 'Social Credit League'. Nineteenth-century Populism in the United States came about because of the failure of the party system to reflect political divisions, but even there the Alliance went through a long period of agonizing before it was prepared to endorse the strategy of becoming a fully-fledged party and competing in elections. It is significant that George Wallace ran in the 1968 presidential election as an independent, and he chastised the existing parties as 'Tweedledum and Tweedledee'. The new populism is characterized and fundamentally motivated by a frustration with parties as both embodying and promoting the type of politics rejected by the new populists. All new populist parties characterize, to some extent, their party systems as closed off from real people and as corrupt unrepresentative cartels.

The dilemma posed by political parties for populism starts from the fact that much of the initial appeal of populism is based on a critique of the politics created by the dominant political parties. As populists gain in support and momentum, they attempt to build on that support by stressing how different they are, and yet the institutional logic of representative politics, in which they operate, forces them to adopt the form of the political party which they critique. Populists, when successful, are forced to become that which they dislike. The result is that populism, in the long term, either becomes less populist (as in the case of Social Credit), or becomes riven with internal conflict (new populism), or simply collapses (the People's Party). Any of these alternatives means that populism is destined to be self-limiting.

Populist, charismatic and authoritarian leadership

One answer to the populist institutional dilemma is to emphasize the role of leaders. In their emphasis on leadership, populists find refuge in embodying virtue in the person of their leaders rather than explicitly tracing out what virtue is. Just as wisdom is whatever resides in the people, so, in the politics of action, the right course becomes that chosen by the right leader. The fusing of personality with principle at the level of leadership is the equivalent of reading off virtue from the residents of the heartland at the level of the movement or the people. The empty heart of populism, the lack of key values, means that it is particularly liable to the politics of personality.

The leadership of many populists can be seen as charismatic. From Juan Perón in Argentina, through William Aberhart in Alberta, to Jean-Marie Le Pen in France, populists have been likely to rely not only on personalized leadership but also on leadership that requires a particular type of personality: a charismatic leader. Weber (1968: 241–5) famously differentiated charismatic authority from traditional and legal-rational forms. He suggested that modern society saw the rise of legal-rational authority as the form where we can trace the legitimacy of leaders through law and institutions and, in democracy, through the consent of the governed. Charismatic authority, unlike traditional authority which traced legitimacy through immemorial traditions, is rooted neither in structures nor in history but in the particular personal characteristics of the leaders and the qualities ascribed to them by their followers (Weber 1968: 244; Willner 1984: 202–3).

There are a number of points of similarity between the concepts of charismatic authority and populism. Charismatic leadership has strong similarities to religious leadership. The term 'charisma' comes from the word 'grace', and charismatic leaders will tend to inspire a loyalty from their followers that is like devotion and is based on faith. As Willner (1984: 7) describes it, the followers of charismatic leaders 'respond to their leader with devotion, awe, reverence, and blind faith, in short, with emotions close to religious worship'. The leaders themselves will be attributed powers that are almost superhuman and which are contrasted with the ordinariness of their followers. Similarly, populism has many echoes of religious movements and is therefore likely to use a form of authority that has echoes of religion. The moral fundamentalism of populist ideas and the often quasi-religious nature of populist movements in practice means that populism is likely to be drawn towards charismatic leaders.

The nature of charismatic leadership is to replace institutions and rules with the will of the charismatic leader. For populists this has consequences. It means that populists do not have to construct layers of institutions. It is their rejection of the institutionalization inherent in representative politics that leads populists to mobilize, and so if they can do this in a way that avoids complex institutional structures then this suits them. The simplicity of the form of charismatic leadership fits well with the populist predisposition towards political and institutional simplicity and directness.

Charismatic authority may arise from times of distress or hardship. Populism, as I have tried to emphasize, appears when its adherents are overcome with a sense of crisis and of moral collapse. In this sense, both populism and charismatic leadership are justified in expedient rather than in universal terms. Or to put it another way, unusual times call for unusual measures or actions. The appearance of individuals with particular personal qualities at times of crisis is likely to be viewed with great relief by their potential followers, as they offer an immediate solution to a situation that is on the edge of impending disaster.

The final similarity between charismatic leadership and populism is that they are both transitory and unstable. Charismatic leadership will tend to transform itself into other forms of authority or it will perish with the individual with which it is associated. The latter is very likely as it is extraordinarily difficult for personalized leadership to be passed on from one individual to another (as they are, obviously enough, not the same person). Where populism relies on charismatic leaders, it has great difficulty in sustaining itself in the long term. Even where it does not rely on charismatic leaders, it still has difficulties in sustaining itself because of its inherent distaste for the institutionalization of politics, and yet institutionalization is one of the prerequisites of survival of any political movement.

Populism has a tendency towards charismatic leadership, but this is indicative of a predilection for strong leadership in general. The charismatic form of leadership is merely symptomatic of the populist simultaneous celebration of the ordinariness of its constituents and the extraordinariness of their leaders. This creates a tension for populism. This tension is sometimes resolved in favour of charismatic leaders, but it is also resolved in favour of authoritarian or semi-authoritarian leadership.

The structure of populist movements and parties is often highly centralized. A whole set of parties that I have called new populist are characterized, to some degree, by structures that they contrast with the bureaucratic model of the mass political party and which therefore tend to be reliant on centralization and personalized leadership. If we look more broadly at the populism of Perón, Perot, Aberhart, Wallace, Long, Glistrup, Bossi, Berlusconi and

Le Pen, they have tended to construct around them parties placing themselves very much at the centre, in organizational and symbolic terms. At the extreme, populist leaders can be extremely intolerant of dissent. Perón's harsh treatment of those opposing his leadership is indicative of this. This intolerance of dissent and the populist tolerance of this intolerance is another indication of the populist rejection of politics. Populism prefers the simple solution of leadership itself over the complex process of politics to resolve problems.

The populist prediction for leadership reflects both a desire to reduce institutional complexity and the embodiment of the populist faith in leadership itself. Both are distinct but lead towards the same end product and help in creating the same dilemmas. The dilemma of leadership for populism is that a movement of ordinary people relies on the most extraordinary of individuals for leadership. At the extreme, these leaders will rely on charisma as the basis of their authority. Where leadership is not charismatic, it tends to be authoritarian or, at least, highly centralized. This comes about because the populists' antipathy towards institutions leads them to attempt to construct simple forms of organization, and that simplicity means the reduction of checks on leadership and so can have the effect of giving great power to whoever heads the structure. Populism is therefore drawn towards a form of leadership that is practically very difficult to sustain in the long term and which is apparently at odds with the celebration of 'the people' as its driving force.

Direct democracy

One of the ways of avoiding or resolving the institutional dilemmas of populism has been to advocate direct democracy as this is a means of both having direct contact with the population and, at the same time, dispensing with political parties. Populism is sometimes portrayed as almost synonymous with direct democracy. While populism has some strong associations with direct democracy, to see the two as nearly synonymous is to underplay the breadth of direct democratic theory and to focus on only one part of populism. Populism can be associated with direct democracy in the sense of advocating a form of politics that, as standard, uses the tools of direct democracy. Populism can also be associated with it as various populist movements have found direct democratic mechanisms to be useful lightning rods for attracting attention to their goals and building up support for their movements.

Direct democracy is used by populists as a critique of the lack of participation in representative democracy (Arblaster 1994) and as an institutional mechanism to add to representative democracy to make it more participatory (Budge 1996). In practice, the mechanisms of direct democracy are used most extensively in Switzerland and in some states in the USA. In both cases they are as adjuncts to the institutions of representative democracy.

In the United States, the development of institutions of direct democracy into the setting of representative politics is often seen as a form of populism. Initiatives, referendums and recall devices have been variously introduced into state settings in order to either supplement or to buttress the representative element of representative politics.

The experience of the use of the initiative in the American states illustrates that it can be a populist tool. In his study of the content of the 399 initiatives in the USA between 1978 and 1992, David Magleby (1994: 238) finds that 76 per cent of them fell into four categories: government or political reform, public morality, revenue or tax or bond, and regulation of business and labour. These categories are instructive because they include the great populist shibboleths of popular morality and distrust of institutions and taxes. One of the most famous initiatives is that of Proposition 13 in California in 1978, which dealt with property taxes and which spurred a flurry of similar tax revolts in other states (Peters 1991: 182–4). The campaign for Proposition 13, led by Howard Jervis, had many populist elements. Jervis was portrayed as a folk hero by the media, and his campaign attacked the politicians and bureaucrats and defended Proposition 13 as amounting to a two-thirds cut in property taxes (Sears and Citrin 1982: 26–31). The incident is famous for the use of the direct democracy tools of the initiative, but what is perhaps more important is the sort of politics that the initiative engendered. The leadership-dependent, anti-elitist, pro-tax-cutting campaign was clearly populist in more than just the mechanism it used.

The use of the institutions of direct democracy does not necessarily mean direct democracy has been instituted, as they are sometimes used to supplement institutions of representative politics. Their use does not necessarily have any relationship to populism. The episodic use of referendums by politicians does not imply an abrogation of their power. Referendums are frequently given the status of consultative mechanisms leaving political elites the possibility of either implementing or ignoring the results given by the people. In so far as direct democracy institutions are constitutionalized, they may embody a populist impulse. This is the case with the use of initiatives in the USA where they have more than an advisory status and represent the real embodiment of a populist strain in US politics.

Conspiracy theories

Another response to populism's institutional dilemmas that does not provide such a practical solution as direct democracy is the tendency to resort to conspiracy theories. The populist tendency to demonize elites and to see danger around them leads them to be particularly susceptible to such theories. Bringing together various elite groups such as bankers, politicians, intellectuals and captains of industry, it is a short step to the claim that they are in cahoots, as part of a conspiracy. Such theories also serve an important mobilizing function. Finding resonance with disgruntled sections of the population, conspiracy theories make sense of what might otherwise be disparate facts of life and, in so doing, provide incentive for individuals to join in the campaign to frustrate whatever conspiracy has been frustrating them.

Conspiracy theories assume that those involved in the conspiracy actively conspire together to further their interests, and do so secretly. Many political science theories suggest both that elites rule and that there is a consistent pattern to the way different sections of the elite participate in this system of rule. These positions characterize democratic elitist theorists who criticize liberal democracies for having power too concentrated in certain social groups (such as Mills 1956) and Marxist and class-based theories that see society as run in the interests of a certain class (Miliband 1969). In their truncated forms, elitist and class-based theories may appear to be conspiracy theories, but they are not. What differentiates these from conspiracy theories is that the system of rule is systematic and institutional rather than the result of the agency or deliberative actions of a small set of individuals. The act of conspiracy does not exist for elite or class-based theories of power as a deliberate act. The circularity of the conspiracy theory is that the conspiracy cannot be detected and so if we cannot see a conspiracy then this is proof that there is one. This means that, by definition, conspiracy theories cannot be rooted out by empirical enquiry. An academic investigation into whether a conspiracy exists is likely, for a conspiracy theorist, to be at best ineffective, and at worst in collusion with the conspiracy. This means that populists have yet another justification in dismissing overly theoretical and academic accounts of power.

The conspiracy is the counter to the heartland. Just as the heartland is an essentially vague and obscure concept but with great resonance, so a conspiracy theory is the iteration of vague threat to the heartland, but one that is both real and profound. It plays a part in adding to a set of myths surrounding the reality of elite rule and justifying populist mobilization.

Conspiracy theories provide populists with an explanation for the problems that populists have in sustaining themselves as political movements and parties. They provide explanations that fit well with the world-view of populism, as it is one step from being opposed to dominant elites to being opposed to secret elites controlling politics. Conspiracy theories are a useful cognitive refuge in the face of institutional dilemmas, but they are not useful mobilizing tools as they stress the relative powerlessness of the populist constituency, the mass of ordinary people.

The episodic nature of populism as a political phenomenon owes much to its highly ambivalent relationship to institutions. This makes it necessarily short-lived. Populism has problems with institutions. At the best of times populists regard institutions with distaste, but at times of crisis they begin to see them as malignant. Coming into politics, populists then have different sorts of problems with institutions. The necessities of institutionalization for the regularization and mobilization of populism as a political force or movement, push populism into the solutions of personalized or centralized leadership or into fragmentation and decomposition. If populists move towards leadership or towards institutionalization they rob themselves of part of their initial appeal or, at least, of a part of their identity. Simply put, they become that which they emerged to challenge.

The attitude towards institutions may also owe something to populism's fundamental ambivalence towards politics as an activity. The populist predisposition seems to be for politics to be done by others. Populists favour the outcome of government over the process of politics. Only under duress do populists form themselves into political movements or parties. One way of looking at this is to see populists as anti-political. Another way is to see this anti-political tone as rooted in the problems they have with institutions. Part of the populist distaste for politics stems from the implicit sense that engagement with institutions, especially the institutions of representative politics, can only end badly for populism.

The ambivalence of populists towards institutions goes some way to explaining why populism in the form of fully-fledged political movements or forces is relatively rare. It causes populism to be self-limiting. At the other extreme, the populist disposition towards institutions also goes some way to explaining the ubiquity of populism as a style or as a rhetorical device. Populism is a convenient tool for the expression of what might be either a passing or an instinctual frustration with political institutions. Any political project or movement will face frustration at some time. Populism is a powerful reference point for those who want to express frustration with political institutions. Such frustration may, in the longer scheme of things, be a passing phase, or an expression of primal political instinct at a time of crisis, and therefore, half-formed if heartfelt, populism provides a convenient alibi and a pedigree for such sentiments. On the one hand populism's institutional ambivalence explains the small number of fully developed populist phenomena, while on the other hand it explains the frequent resort to populism as half-formed sentiment or as tone or style by politicians of all ideological colours.

10
Populism and Representative Politics

Democracy is *the* dominant political idea of our age. It is easy (and almost accurate) to declare that 'we are all democrats now'. There is a difference in whether this refers to the idea or the institutions of democracy. The modern prevalence of the idea of democracy is due to some very different conceptions of the idea. In other words, there is such apparently wide agreement in the virtues of democracy because such different meanings are attached to the term. Disguising the inevitable range of differences in key values and interpretations of how the world works, democracy treads a wide path across that range. It is in the very nature of key political concepts that they are 'essentially contested concepts', that we should expect dispute and debate about their meaning, and democracy is classically contested in this way (Gallie 1962).

In the institutions of democratic politics – in other words, in the way the idea is put into practice – there is more of a measure of agreement. If we try and draw up the list of what institutions and practices come with democracy, it is possible to see a widely (and, in this case, genuinely) held consensus that democracy is characterized by such features as a mass franchise allowing voters the opportunity to choose between competitive political parties to send to assemblies, parliaments and councils. For some these are minimal requirements, while for others they are seen as in themselves constituting democracy. Whatever their status, implicit in the acceptance of the institutions is the prevalence of the representative model of democracy. Modern democratic politics is, in practice, almost invariably representative democratic politics.

Representative democracy, with the easily identifiable form of elections, assemblies and political parties, has become the measure of democracy for many. These have become the toolbox of democracy. Although the tools are put to some very different uses, it is remarkable that so many and such different politicians, movements and regimes attempt to build their legitimacy through their use. Leaders build parties around them for legitimacy. Regimes construct elections to legitimize governments. International institutions like the European Union use the institutional equipment of representative politics as a prerequisite for membership.

The prevalence of representative democratic institutions is bound up with the fate of liberalism. Ideas of the rights of citizens, of the limits of the state, of the rule of law permeate much of modern politics. Combining these with the institutions of representative politics, it is possible to perceive that liberal ideas seem to have an almost hegemonic status. Some greet this with enthusiasm, declaring, most famously, the 'end of history' in the triumph of liberalism, while others portray the development as sinister and as a smokescreen for the 'free market' and inevitable inequalities of power and wealth.

Populism as reaction to representative politics

'Representative politics', as a term, describes the type of politics that occurs around the institutions of liberal democracy. Of course there are varieties of representative politics, since different political systems have different institutional constellations and different political norms and values according to the national or local setting, but it is still useful for us to identify a sort of politics that occurs in democracies designed around representation.

There is a range of processes that make up representative politics. Representative politics is made up of a set of interacting and independent processes including electoral cycles, party politics, public debate, and public policy making. Through these cycles and processes, ideas are articulated, implications iterated, ideas and their implications contested with other ideas, and selected ideas implemented in the form of public policy.

In a very abstract way, it is possible to characterize populism as the embodiment of a primal political reaction of the ruled against the rulers. It would only be very abstract because such a phenomenon would have a huge range within it, and because populism can only be populism once it finds articulation in a systematic set of ideas. The processes of representative politics involve the process of systematically developing and promoting political programmes and thereby constituting the ideas that become populist. For populism to become a political movement it has to be structured against and through the processes of representative politics.

The cases of populism examined in Part One illustrate the reaction to representative politics. Part of the very identity of the Russian *narodniki* was bound up with their belief in the possibility of a Russian path to revolution, and this was *de facto* a rejection of prevailing ideas of democracy as a revolutionary idea. Their championing of the institutions of the Russian peasantry was an explicit rejection of the institutions associated with representative politics. With the populist ideas of Social Credit in Alberta, the aim of establishing an essentially technocratic board to oversee both the functioning of the economy and the distribution of social justice was a profound repudiation of representative politics. It took away the competence from the people (or their elected representatives) and also amounted to an attempt to bypass any sort of politics or political process that might be associated with the making of public policy. It was an attempt to take politics out of policy making, whereas the logic of representative politics is to build politics into policy making.

In the case of Peronism, I have stressed the importance of leadership. Perón can be seen as symptomatic of a tendency towards charismatic or personalized leadership. The relationship between leadership and representative politics is complex because of the tension between leading and following mass opinions. We can say that personalized or charismatic leadership is contrary to representative politics because it leads to a reversal of the relationship between masses and their representatives. With charismatic leadership followers follow because of who the leaders are, whereas in representative politics leaders are chosen on the basis of who they represent.

The new populism reflects at least an ambivalence towards representative politics. New populist parties are protest parties. Part of the new populist critique of contemporary politics focuses on the overrepresentation of minorities. Believing the state to be in hock to either organized interests or a liberal elite consensus, new populism attacks contemporary representative politics as dysfunctional. New populism has both specific critiques of the functioning of representative politics and a diffuse but powerful sense of dissatisfaction with politics.

If populism has, as I suggest, its roots in a reaction of the ruled against the rulers, it has two implications. The first is that populism, at root, is unformed and diffuse. The manifestations of this feeling can take very different forms. As a vague sense is translated into political actions or political ideas (or both) it will feed into different sets of already held assumptions and into some fundamentally different contexts, and will consequently look very different. The structuring effects of different systems of representative politics will thereby give rise to different variants of populism.

The second implication is that populism is *not* a reaction against modernity. This goes against the grain for many analyses of populism that have portrayed it as having its roots in a reactionary response to modernization (see for example, Lipset 1963). The connection between populism and modernity is more complex than a simple link. Modernity allows the conditions for populism to become systematized and therefore to become manifest in populist movements. At the same time, modernity does exacerbate the populist sense of frustration against being ruled, by creating complex forms of politics and institutional structures. These become targets of populist angst.

The scale of modern societies is another factor that contributes to the emergence of populism. With a greater scale comes a greater potential distance between the rulers and the ruled and, more importantly, it encourages the tendency to abstract the rulers and the ruled. Regarding a feudal landlord as oppressive is one thing, but it becomes another thing all together when the landlord is generalized to a class of individuals. Populism emerges when 'he' becomes 'they'. In a parallel fashion, 'I' becomes 'we' as the people are invoked as a generalized entity subject to the same conditions and frustrations as the individual.

The contemporary context of politics increases the scope, the scale and complexity of representation. International institutions such as the European Union have developed and created new arenas of politics, and at the same time have stretched out the potential scope of representation for individuals. The simple act of voting is rarely in modern politics a single act, as voting and representation take place simultaneously at a number of levels: local, national and international. This increase in scope and complexity of representative politics provides more scope for representation and it also provides more possibilities and sources of populism.

Populism and its impact on representative politics

The relationship of populism to representative politics is not one-way. It is possible to trace some effects that populist movements have on the system of representative politics into which they emerge. Populist movements have particular effects on the politics of representative systems. The populist rhetorical preoccupation with 'the people' (albeit, as we have seen in Chapter 8, a particular conception of the people) means that it draws on one of the key touchstones of representative democracy. It is not unusual in this. Most movements in representative politics will claim to be of the people in some way. However, in the way that it pits the people explicitly against the elites, populism transforms what can otherwise be a rather bland rallying cry into a potent political weapon.

Populism, by its very presence in a system of representative politics, creates a context which transforms the relationship between politicians and people. Shils suggests that populism inserts an 'inverted egalitarianism' because it 'is tinged by the belief that the people are not just the equal of their rulers; they are actually better than their rulers' (Shils 1956: 101). This transforms the basis by which other institutions of representation can claim their legitimacy and can make claims about public policy. Populism has the effect of structuring political debate in three ways: through the politics of simplicity, popular sovereignty and dichotomy.

Populism aims to create a politics of simplicity. Politics should embody the wisdom of the simple people and therefore should itself be simple and direct. By the very expression of this claim it partially succeeds. Other parties or movements are forced to reconstitute their positions both in opposition to populist claims but also in imitation of the simple style of populism. Populism's presence thereby has the effect of delegitimizing complex or technical policy initiatives.

Populism tends to define the vocabulary of political debate. This feature owes much to the spread of democracy as an idea. Given that populism invariably claims to speak in the name of the people (the heartland's population), there is a congruence between these types of claim and the demands of democracy that politics is legitimized in so far as it embodies popular sovereignty. This means that although populism's commitment to 'the people' is, at best, a vague claim, it has the effect of legitimising populist claims.

The final effect of populism on political debate is that it

dichotomizes issues, forcing them to be couched in either pro and anti terms. Inherent in populism is the tendency towards political dualism. This is partly the result of an attempt to construct simple politics that can allow direct representation, but is also symptomatic of a something deeper in populism. The dualism is another way of seeing the polarizing of elites and masses as a whole. Both are portrayed as relatively monolithic, and just as populism is reluctant to see divisions between elites because such niceties obscure the fundamental unity of purpose and interest of elites, so they are reluctant to differentiate and divide 'the people'. The broad parameters of the elites and the people are heavily drawn, but the detail within those categories is noticeably absent.

The framing of the political world in dualist terms by populism applies to issues as much as to interests. Just as the political world is divided into two competing forces, it makes sense to then read off political issues in the same terms. Politics becomes dualized in terms of both the players and the play. This makes for the simple politics of good and bad, of right and wrong. It also explains why populists seem so easily to spill from the secular to moral fundamentalism and quasi-religious imagery.

The complexity of society and of the decisions it has to take is part of the rationale for democratic politics. The particular use of representative democracy is symptomatic of this. The most intuitive reasons for having representatives make decisions is not the negative one that people should not themselves make these decisions (indeed, all democrats would agree that ideally they should) but that it is necessary that some individuals be exclusively dedicated to making those decisions. The need for representatives implies that the demands of politics are such that they are inconsistent with the activities that otherwise make us worthy of making those decisions. To be 'the people' means that we must be engaged in constitutive acts – of work, of home – and therefore unable to be exclusively dedicated to politics.

Representative politics allows the expression of a range of political positions. Indeed, it is premised on the multiplicity of such positions and serves as mechanism for creating public policy through the contestation of the advantages and disadvantages of these positions. Populism has a somewhat different status from other ideologies that stems from its roots as a reaction to those institutions themselves rather than to the debate within the institutions. It is deeply rooted in the processes and practices of representative politics but only occasionally finds systematic expression.

The irony of populism is that the system that causes institutional frustration offers the systematic means of representing and building support for that frustration. While populism may be present in nuance in non-democratic systems, it is only when the opportunity exists for structuring diffuse populist sentiment into political movements or parties that populism comes into its own. And yet, part of the protest element of populism comes from the sentiment that the very system of representative politics is found wanting.

In its most 'extreme' forms, populism can be in danger of spilling over into authoritarianism and away from democracy. We see this in the practices of Peronism and in the structures of some new populist parties. Populism therefore tests the tolerance of representative politics. However, it is notable that all the cases of populism dealt with in this book justify themselves in terms of how far they represent the people (however defined) and have all, with the exception of the Russian *narodniki*, contested elections and formed themselves as parties.

11

Conclusion

It is important that we get populism right. In part this is because the term is used so widely and in such a cavalier manner, and so it is important to focus it either so that it has real meaning or so that at least the debate around it has real meaning. But there is a reason that goes beyond the intellectual niceties of conceptual precision and debate. Populism is used so widely as a term because it *is* a phenomenon that is ubiquitous in modern politics. Admittedly populism is only occasionally translated into significant political movements or parties, but it permeates representative politics as always a potential force. Being alive to the possibility of populism will give us a more vital insight into contemporary representative politics.

We must understand populism because to do so is to make fuller our comprehension of those ideologies that attach themselves to populism. The empty heart of populism is invariably remedied with values of other ideologies. To understand the content of those ideologies we must understand populism as a component part.

I have deliberately tried to avoid portraying populism as good or bad. It is easy to dismiss populist panaceas as either unrealistic or as positively dangerous. However, this does not necessarily mean that we should dismiss populist movements out of hand. Populism is a gauge by which we can measure the health of representative political systems. Where populists, as inherently politically reluctant, mobilize as movements or parties, there are strong grounds for examining the functioning of representative politics and for suspecting that all may not be well. This does not necessarily mean that we need accept the populist solutions but it does mean that we should be sensitive to the presence of populism. The fragmentary and rather scarce conceptualization of populism within the social sciences does not help us in this.

The hegemony of representative politics and its institutions reflects the power of liberal ideas. Liberalism emerged as a set of ideas to defend the citizen from the state and to give the state popular consent as its basis. If we look at some of the core ideas of liberalism, it is clear that populism, in its widest sense, is a reaction against it. Liberalism has a world-view that is constructed around individuals. Populism deals in collectivities in its celebration of the people as an organic whole. Liberalism further imbues individuals with rights as one way of defending them from unwarranted state intrusion into their freedom. Populism is hostile to a discourse of rights because, by definition, rights are tools of the embattled minority, while populism sees the majority as embattled and blames the excessive deference of the state to rights claims of minorities for this injustice. Liberalism instinctively prefers the market over the state as the form of economic regulation. Populism has had no qualms about state involvement in the economy and, further, has a tendency to allow regimes that it favours to be authoritarian and therefore potentially highly interventionist.

Populism is an intermittent but recurrent reaction to liberalism. As such it is one among many. If we are prepared to transcend a simple and rather time-bound conception of politics as a set of ideas spread along a left–right continuum, other reactions to liberalism come into clear relief. Nationalism and religious fundamentalism offer profound and abiding challenges to liberalism and its politics. These ideologies differ from populism in having delineated constituencies. Indeed, they arise out of powerful identifications with national or ethnic groups or out of faith. Populism has the task of constructing itself as an entity out of reaction to representative politics. The raw material for this exercise are 'the people', and the resonance of this concept with the rhetoric of representative politics is fortuitous for populism.

The politics of liberalism is embodied in the practices, procedures and structures of representative politics. Populism grows from, into and out of representative politics. It is something of an irony that populism is given the capacity to maintain itself in the form of systematic political movements only under systems of representative politics but that the impetus for populism comes from frustration with representative politics.

Apart from the almost hegemonic status of liberal ideas,

contemporary politics sees some major changes. Modern politics sees the construction of significant political institutions no longer tied to the nation-state. The structures and the politics of entities such as the European Union have strong state-like qualities but defy categorizations as either substitute nation-states or international institutions. The increased scale of these institutions means not that the representative politics of nation-states is usurped or rendered obsolete. Rather it means that the scope and complexity of representative politics are increased. This heightens the possibility of populism as a reaction to new forms of representative politics.

The form and structure of political parties as the linkage mechanisms of representative politics have also changed. If we look at parties as institutions of political association that have linked leaders, as representatives, to electors, as the represented, through a core of activists, the balance of power has shifted. Parties have become hollowed out, with the activist core being both downgraded and minimized. Using the mass media and access to wealth, single individuals can construct parties with relative ease and with remarkable speed and effectiveness. Contemporary populists, such as Perot and Berlusconi, have taken full advantage of the possibilities this change affords.

If we return to some of the themes I identified in Chapter 1, it is clear that a changed context of contemporary politics has increased the scope for populism. The prevalence of representative democratic institutions at a national level and the attempt to introduce them at supranational level means that populists, as hostile to representative politics, have more potential sources of grievance. Through globalization and the associated uncertainties of identity that come about with the construction (imagined or real) of a 'global community' there will be more impetus for those feeling excluded to take refuge in an imagined heartland. This will be true especially in so far as a sense of crisis is increasingly felt by those excluded from the new global community. We already see this, in nuance, with the resort by some groups to a sense of ethnic or national identity as a bulwark against real or imagined global forces. An increasing scale of politics means that the grip of more specific ideologies is loosened in the public imagination, and populism has a greater range of ideological partners with which it can fuse. Its chameleonic character means that populism can be indicative of a wider problem with representative politics and yet, in each case, it will bear the strong imprimatur of its political context.

Understanding populism properly means that we are more likely to identify and understand its self-limiting nature. If we support populist movements then we will need to think of new ways out of its institutional dilemmas. If we are opposed to populist movements then we may take comfort from the knowledge that new ways out of old but profound dilemmas are hard to come by. Either way, it is important that we understand populism as it is a way of understanding the representative politics which is so prevalent around us.

References

Allcock, J.B. (1971) 'Populism': a brief biography, *Sociology*, 5: 371–87.

Andersen, J.G. (1992) Denmark: The Progress Party – populist neo-liberalism and welfare state chauvinism, in P. Hainsworth (ed.) *The Extreme Right in Europe and the USA*. London: Pinter.

Anderson, K., Berman, R.A., Luke, T., Piccone, P. and Taves, M. (1991) The Empire Strikes Out: a roundtable on populist politics, *Telos*, 87: 3–70.

Arblaster, A. (1994) *Democracy*, 2nd edn. Buckingham: Open University Press.

Bell, D. (ed.) (1963) *The Radical Right*. New York: Anchor.

Berlin, I. (1978) *Russian Thinkers*. London: Hogarth Press.

Berlin, I., Hofstadter, R., MacRae, D. *et al.* (1968) To define populism, *Government and Opposition*, 3: 137–79.

Betz, H.-G. (1994) *Radical Right-Wing Populism in Western Europe*. New York: St Martin's Press.

Betz, H.-G. (1998) Introduction, in H.-G. Betz and S. Immerfall (eds) *The New Politics of the Right: Neo-Populist Parties and Movements in Established Democracies*. Basingstoke: Macmillan.

Budge, I. (1996) *The New Challenge of Direct Democracy*. Cambridge: Polity.

Burnham, W.D. (1970) *Critical Elections and the Mainsprings of American Politics*. New York: W.W. Norton.

Canovan, M. (1981) *Populism*. London: Junction.

Canovan, M. (1982) Two strategies for the study of populism, *Political Studies*, 30: 544–52.

Canovan, M. (1984) 'People', politicians and populism, *Government and Opposition*, 19: 312–27.

Canovan, M. (1999) Trust the people! Populism and the two faces of democracy, *Political Studies*, 47: 2–16.

Carter, D.T. (1995) *The Politics of Rage: George Wallace, the Origins of the New Conservatism, and the Transformation of American Politics*. New York: Simon & Schuster.

Cheles, L., Ferguson, R. and Vaughan, M. (eds) (1995) *The Far Right in Western and Eastern Europe*, 2nd edn. Harlow: Longman.

Conniff, M.L. (1999) Brazil's populist republic and beyond, in M.L. Conniff (ed.) *Populism in Latin America*. Tuscaloosa: University of Alabama Press.

Conway, J.F. (1978) Populism in the United States, Russia and Canada: Explaining the roots of Canada's third parties, *Canadian Journal of Political Science*, 11: 99–124.

Crasweller, R.D. (1987) *Perón and the Enigmas of Argentina*. New York: W.W. Norton.

Di Tella, T.S. (1965) Populism and reform in Latin America, in C. Veliz (ed.) *Obstacles to Change in Latin America*. Oxford: Oxford University Press.

Di Tella, T.S. (1997) Populism in the twenty-first century, *Government and Opposition*, 32: 187–200.

Dulles, J.F.W. (1967) *Vargas of Brazil: A Political Biography*. Austin: University of Texas Press.

Eatwell, R. (1982) Poujadism and neo-Poujadism: from revolt to reconciliation, in P. Cerny (ed.) *Social Movements and Protest in France*. London: Frances Pinter.

Gallie, W.B. (1962) Essentially contested concepts, in M. Black (ed.) *The Importance of Language*. Englewood Cliffs, NJ: Prentice Hall.

Gentile, P. and Kriesi, H. (1998) Contemporary radical-right parties in Switzerland: history of a divided family, in H.-G. Betz and S. Immerfall (eds) *The New Politics of the Right: Neo-Populist Parties and Movements in Established Democracies*. Basingstoke: Macmillan.

Germani, G. (1978) *Authoritarianism, Fascism, and National Populism*. New Brunswick, NJ: Transaction.

Gold, H.J. (1995) Third party voting in presidential elections: a study of Perot, Anderson and Wallace, *Political Research Quarterly*, 48: 751–74.

Goodwyn, L. (1976) *Democratic Promise: The Populist Movement in America*. New York: Oxford University Press.

Grant, S.A. (1976) *Obschina* and *mir*, *Slavic Review*, 35: 636–51.

Hair, W.I. (1991) *The Kingfish and his Realm: The Life and Times of Huey P. Long*. Baton Rouge: Louisiana State University Press.

Hainsworth, P. (ed.) (1992) *The Extreme Right in Europe and the USA*. London: Pinter.

Harris, G. (1990) *The Dark Side of Europe*. Edinburgh: Edinburgh University Press.

Hayward, J. (1996) The populist challenge to elitist democracy in Europe, in J. Hayward (ed.) *Elitism, Populism, and European Politics*. Oxford: Clarendon.

Hicks, J.D. (1961) *The Populist Revolt: A History of the Farmers' Alliance and the People's Party*. Lincoln: University of Nebraska Press.

Hine, D. (1996) Political parties and the public accountability of leaders, in J. Hayward (ed.) *Elitism, Populism and European Politics*. Oxford: Clarendon.

Hoffman, S. (1956) *Le Mouvement Poujade*. Paris: Librarie Armand Colin.

Hofstadter, R. (1955) *The Age of Reform*. New York: Alfred A. Knopf.

Husbands, C.T. (1992) Belgium: Flemish legions on the march, in P. Hainsworth (ed.) *The Extreme Right in Europe and the USA*. London: Pinter.

Ignazi, P. (1992) The silent counter-revolution: hypotheses on the emergence of extreme right-wing parties in Europe, *European Journal of Political Research*, 22: 3–34.

Ignazi, P. (1996) The transformation of the MSI into the AN, *West European Politics*, 19: 693–714.

Immerfall, S. (1998) The neo-populist agenda, in H.-G. Betz and S. Immerfall (eds) *The New Politics of the Right: Neo-Populist Parties and Movements in Established Democracies*. Basingstoke: Macmillan.

Ionescu, G. and Gellner, E. (eds) (1969a) *Populism: Its Meaning and National Characteristics*. London: Weidenfeld and Nicolson.

Ionescu, G. and Gellner, E. (1969b) Introduction, in G. Ionescu and E. Gellner (eds) *Populism: Its Meanings and National Characteristics*. London: Weidenfeld and Nicolson.

Irving, J.A. (1959) *The Social Credit Movement in Alberta*. Toronto: University of Toronto Press.

Johnson, C. (1998) Pauline Hanson and One Nation, in H.-G. Betz and S. Immerfall (eds) *The New Politics of the Right: Neo-Populist Parties and Movements in Established Democracies*. Basingstoke: Macmillan.

Kazin, M. (1995) *The Populist Persuasion: An American History*. New York: Basic Books.

Kitching, G. (1989) *Development and Underdevelopment in Historical Perspective: Populism, Nationalism and Industrialization*, rev. edn. London: Routledge.

Kitschelt, H. (in collaboration with A. J. McGann) (1995) *The Radical Right in Western Europe: A Comparative Analysis*. Ann Arbor: University of Michigan Press.

Kornhauser, W. (1959) *The Politics of Mass Society*. London: Routledge & Kegan Paul.

Kumar, K. (1991) *Utopianism*. Buckingham: Open University Press.

Laclau, E. (1977) *Politics and Ideology in Marxist Theory*. London: Verso.

Lasch, C. (1991) *The True and Only Heaven: Progress and Its Critics*, New York: W.W. Norton.

Laycock, D. (1994) Reforming Canadian democracy? Institutions and ideology in the Reform Party project, *Canadian Journal of Political Science*, 27: 213–47.

LeDuc, L. (1994) The Canadian federal election of 1993, *Electoral Studies*, 13: 163–8.

Lesher, S. (1994) *George Wallace: American Populist*. Reading, MA: Addison-Wesley.

Levine, R.M. (1970) *The Vargas Regime: The Critical Years, 1934–1938*. New York: Columbia University Press.

Levitas, R. (1990) *The Concept of Utopia*. New York: Philip Allan.

Lipset, S.M. (1963) *Political Man: The Social Bases of Support*. New York: Anchor.

Lipset, S.M. and Raab, E. (1971) *The Politics of Unreason: Right-Wing Extremism in America, 1790–1970*. London: Heinemann.

Long, H. (1933) *Every Man a King: The Autobiography of Huey P. Long*. New Orleans: National Book Co.

Luther, K.R. (1992) Consociationalism, parties and the party system, *West European Politics*, 15: 45–98.

McCann, J.A., Rapoport, R.B. and Stone, W.J. (1999) Heeding the call: an assessment of mobilization into H. Ross Perot's 1992 presidential campaign, *American Journal of Political Science*, 43: 1–28.

McCarthy, P. (1996) *Forza Italia*: the overwhelming success and the consequent problems of a virtual party, in R.S. Katz and P. Ignazi (eds) *Italian Politics: The Year of the Tycoon*. Boulder, CO: Westview.

McGuigan J. (1992) *Cultural Populism*. London: Routledge.

Macpherson, C.B. (1962) *Democracy in Alberta: Social Credit and the Party System*, 2nd edn. Toronto: University of Toronto Press.

Magleby, D.B. (1994) Direct legislation in the American States, in D. Butler and A. Ranney (eds) *Referendums Around the World: The Growing Use of Direct Democracy*. Basingstoke: Macmillan.

Malloy, J.M. (1977) Authoritarianism and corporatism in Latin America: the modal pattern, in J.M. Malloy (ed.) *Authoritarianism and Corporatism in Latin America*. Pittsburgh: University of Pittsburgh Press.

Mény, Y. (1998) *The People, the Elites and the Populist Challenge*, Jean Monnet Chair Papers. Florence: European University Institute.

Merkl, P.H. and Weinberg, L. (eds) (1993) *Encounters with the Contemporary Radical Right*. Boulder, CO: Westview.

Mills, C.W. (1956) *The Power Elite*. Oxford: Oxford University Press.

Miliband, R. (1969) *The State in Capitalist Society*. London: Weidenfeld & Nicolson.

Mouzelis, N. (1985) On the concept of populism: populist and clientelist modes of incorporation in semi-peripheral politics, *Politics & Society*, 14: 329–48.

Newell, J.L. and Bull, M. (1997) Party organisations and alliances in Italy in the 1990s: a revolution of sorts, *West European Politics*, 20: 81–109.

Nugent, W.T.K. (1963) *The Tolerant Populists: Kansas Populism and Nativism*. Chicago: University of Chicago Press.

Page, J.A. (1983) *Perón: A Biography*. New York: Random House.

People's Party (1978) The Omaha Platform, July 1892, in G.B. Tindall (ed.)

A Populist Reader: Selections from the Works of American Populist Leaders. Glouster, MA: Peter Smith.

Peters, B.G. (1991) *The Politics of Taxation: A Comparative Perspective.* Oxford: Blackwell.

Piccone, P. (1991) The crisis of liberalism and the emergence of federal populism, *Telos*, 89: 7–44.

Piccone, P. (1995) Postmodern populism, *Telos*, 103: 45–86.

Pipes, R. (1964) Narodnichestvo: a semantic inquiry, *Slavic Review*, 23: 441–58.

Pipes, R. (1995) *Russia under the Old Regime*, 2nd edn. London: Penguin.

Richards, J. (1981) Populism: a qualified defence, *Studies in Political Economy*, 5: 5–27.

Riedlsperger, M. (1998) The Freedom Party of Austria: from protest to radical right populism, in H. Betz and S. Immerfall (eds) *The New Politics of the Right: Neo-Populist Parties and Movements in Established Democracies.* Basingstoke: Macmillan.

Ritter, G. (1997) *Goldbugs and Greenbacks: The Antimonopoly Tradition and the Politics of Finance in America, 1865–1896.* Cambridge: Cambridge University Press.

Rock, D. (1986) *Argentina 1516–1982: From Spanish Colonization to the Falklands War.* London: Tauris.

Rogin, M.P. (1967) *The Intellectuals and McCarthy: The Radical Specter.* Cambridge, MA: MIT Press.

Sears, D.O. and Citrin, J. (1982) *Tax Revolt: Something for Nothing in California.* Cambridge, MA: Harvard University Press.

Seisselberg, J. (1996) *Forza Italia*: a 'media-mediated personality-party', *West European Politics*, 19: 715–43.

Seton-Watson, H. (1967) *The Russian Empire 1801–1917.* Oxford: Clarendon Press.

Shils, E. (1956) *The Torment of Secracy: The Background and Consequences of American Security Policies.* Glencoe, IL: Free Press.

Shils, E. (1962) The intellectuals in the political development of the new states, in J.H. Kautsky (ed.) *Political Change in Underdeveloped Countries: Nationalism and Communism.* New York: Wiley.

Smith, W.S. (1983) The return of Peronism, in F.C. Turner and J.E. Miguens (eds) *Juan Perón and the Reshaping of Argentina.* Pittsburgh: University of Pittsburgh Press.

Svåsand, L. (1998) Scandinavian right-wing radicalism, in H.-G. Betz and S. Immerfall (eds) *The New Politics of the Right: Neo-Populist Parties and Movements in Established Democracies.* Basingstoke: Macmillan.

Swyngedouw, M. (1998) The extreme right in Belgium: Of a non-existent Front National and an Omnipresent Vlaams Blok, in H.-G. Betz and S. Immerfall (eds) *The New Politics of the Right: Neo-Populist Parties and Movements in Established Democracies.* Basingstoke: Macmillan.

Taggart, P. (1995) New populist parties in Western Europe, *West European Politics*, 18: 34–51.

Taggart, P. (1996) *The New Populism and the New Politics: New Protest Parties in Sweden in a Comparative Perspective*. Basingstoke: Macmillan.

Taguieff, P.-A. (1995) Political science confronts populism, *Telos*, 103: 9–43.

Telos (1991) Populism vs the new class: the second Elizabethtown *Telos* conference, *Telos*, 88: 2–155.

Telos (1991–92) Special Section on the Leagues in Italy, *Telos*, 903–88.

Telos (1995a) Special Issue on Populism I, *Telos*, 103.

Telos (1995b) Special Issue on Populism II, *Telos*, 104.

Ulam, A.B. (1981) *Russian's Failed Revolutions: From the Decembrists to the Dissidents*. London: Weidenfeld and Nicolson.

Ulam, A.B. (1998) *Prophets and Conspirators in Prerevolutionary Russia*. New Brunswick, NJ: Transaction.

Venturi, F. (1960) *Roots of Revolution: A History of the Populist and Socialist Movements in Nineteenth-Century Russia*. London: Weidenfeld and Nicolson.

Walicki, A. (1969) *The Controversy over Capitalism: Studies in the Social Philosophy of the Russian Populists*. Oxford: Clarendon Press.

Walicki, A. (1980) *A History of Russian Thought from the Enlightenment to Marxism*. Oxford: Clarendon.

Weber, M. (1968) *Economy and Society*, Vol. 1, edited by G. Roth and C. Wittich. New York: Bedminster Press.

Westlind, D. (1996) *The Politics of Popular Identity: Understanding Recent Populist Movements in Sweden and the United States*. Lund: Lund University Press.

Wiles, P. (1969) A syndrome, not a doctrine: some elementary theses on populism, in G. Ionescu and E. Gellner (eds) *Populism: Its Meanings and National Characteristics*. London: Weidenfeld and Nicolson.

Willner, A.R. (1984) *The Spellbinders: Charismatic Political Leadership*. New Haven, CT: Yale University Press.

Winkler, J.R. and Schumann, S. (1998) Radical right-wing parties in contemporary Germany, in H.-G. Betz and S. Immerfall (eds) *The New Politics of the Right: Neo-Populist Parties and Movements in Established Democracies*. Basingstoke: Macmillan.

Worsley, P. (1969) The concept of populism, in G. Ionescu and E. Gellner (eds) *Populism: Its Meanings and National Characteristics*. London: Weidenfeld and Nicolson.

Wortman, R. (1967) *The Crisis of Russian Populism*. Cambridge: Cambridge University Press.

Index

POSTCOMMUNISM

Richard Sakwa

- Is there such a thing as postcommunism?
- What are the central elements of the concept?
- What does postcommunism mean for us all?

Postcommunism has joined the list of terms like postmodernity and postcolonialism that defines the spirit of our age. Designed for undergraduate courses and an essential reference for those more familiar with the field, this authoritative text examines the validity and ramifications of the concept and places it in the broader context of global change. The emergence of communism was accompanied by the development of a critical body of thinking that questioned the basic assumptions of revolutionary socialism and that ultimately proved to be communism's downfall. Sakwa shows how the apparent exhaustion of the revolutionary socialist alternative poses new challenges to the hegemony of the capitalist order itself. He examines the historical origins of postcommunism and its practice in countries that had previously been communist, and situates it in a larger theoretical perspective, focusing on the challenge of finding adequate forms for political and national community in an increasingly fragmented world.

Contents
Introduction: defining postcommunism – The long transcendence – The communist experience – Postcommunism in practice – Coming to terms with communism – Paradoxes and paradigms – Postcommunism in perspective – Notes – Index.

160 pp   0 335 20057 5 (paperback)   0 335 20058 3 (hardback)

ORIENTALISM

Ziauddin Sardar

- Why did Orientalism emerge and how has it evolved?
- Has the theory of Orientalism developed by Edward Said and others stood the test of time?
- What is the significance of postmodernism for the future of Orientalism?

Orientalism, the theory and practice of representing 'the Orient', is a controversial and a problematic concept. This book provides a concise text on the evolution and development of the theory of Orientalism, the practice of Orientalism in history, and its persistence and reformulation in contemporary times. It places Edward Said's contribution in an appropriate historical context, examines the work of his critics, and explores the postmodern future of Orientalism. Ziauddin Sardar provides a highly original historical perspective and shows how Orientalism was reworked and reinvested during the Middle Ages, the Enlightenment, colonialism and under the impact of modernity. Through the examination of a wide range of cultural products – films, television, fiction, CD-Roms – the book argues that, as a practice of representing the 'Other', Orientalism has been substantially transformed: it has reformulated itself as a far more diverse as well as a more sophisticated tool of representation.

Contents
Preface – The concept of orientalism – A short history – Theory and criticism – The contemporary practice – The postmodern future – Notes – Select bibliography – Index.

144 pp   0 335 20206 3 (Paperback)   0 335 20207 1 (Hardback)

POSTMODERNITY

David Lyon

Postmodernity as idea, critique, cultural experience and social condition has engendered a huge, sometimes angry, sometimes anxious debate across the social sciences and humanities. David Lyon provides a stimulating introduction to this contested concept. Seeing postmodernity as a multilayered concept that alerts us to a variety of major changes taking place at the end of the twentieth century means several key processes are implicated: rapid technological change, shifting political concerns, the rise of social movements and globalization. But the question is even bigger: is modernity itself, as a social-cultural entity, disintegrating – including the whole grand edifice of Enlightenment rationality and progress? Is a new type of society emerging structured around consumers and consumption rather than workers and production?

David Lyon traces the lineage of the concept, the key thinkers in its 'development' and possible futures. He explores its relationship to postmodernism in the arts, whether it might be placed as an end of millenium phenomenon, if the judgment that we are already in a postmodern condition is premature, and how some aspects of modern *and* premodern culture are still available and viable. This is an accessible and enjoyable 'tourist' guide around the complex and sometimes exotic territory of postmodernity.

> *Postmodernity* offers a lucid critical guide to the current debate over the transformation of modern conditions. Through a wide ranging and finely tuned analysis of the postmodern configuration David Lyon provides a stimulating introduction to one of the most controversial contemporary concerns.
>
> (Barry Smart)

Contents

112 pp   0 335 19148 7 (Paperback)

ECOLOGISM
TOWARDS ECOLOGICAL CITIZENSHIP

Mark J. Smith

- How should we understand nature and the environment?
- What does it mean to be responsible for the environment?
- Are social and political theories 'anthropocentric' and if the answer is yes, how do we change them?

Ecological thinking within social and political theory has taken off in the past three decades. Green movements have had a dramatic impact upon political and social life, provoking conflicts of interest over major areas of public policy. This reader-friendly text examines the challenges of ecological thought for the assumptions within the traditions of social and political theory. Ecological concerns are often grafted onto existing approaches, but this book examines how the fundamental questions raised by a green perspective transform the terms of reference of modern thinking.

Mark J. Smith outlines the distinctive features of ecological thought and examines two contentious areas of environmental ethics: the obligations for present generations to future generations and the relationship of human to non-human animals. Through these case studies, the author highlights some of the difficulties and contradictions of applying conventional ideas of rights and justice to environmental issues, pointing the way to a new politics of obligation grounded upon ecological citizenship. Designed as an invaluable student text in environmental studies, politics and sociology, this book is essential reading for those with a wider interest in ecology and the environment.

Contents

Introduction: understanding nature – Obligations to future generations and intergenerational justice – Human and non-human animals – Ecology, individualism and the social order – The environment and human emancipation – The prospects for ecological citizenship – References – Index.

120 pp   0 335 19603 9 (paperback)   0 335 19604 7 (hardback)